The Ultimate Guide to
WOODWORKING WITH RESIN

Step-by-Step Instructions, Tips, Techniques and Projects

GABRIEL ANDREWS

Copyright @ 2023 by Gabriel Andrews

All rights reserved. This book or any portion thereof may not be reproduced or used in any manner whatsoever without the express written permission of the publisher except for the use of brief quotations in a book review.

CONTENTS

INTRODUCTION 8

CHAPTER 1: WOODWORKING WITH RESIN 12
- Materials and Tools 12
- Types of Resin 15
- Resin Techniques 15
- Tips for Working with Resin 17

CHAPTER 2: ESSENTIAL TOOLS AND MATERIALS FOR WOODWORKING WITH RESIN 20
- Mixing cups and stir sticks 21
- Sanding materials 22
- Woodworking tools 24

CHAPTER 3: PREPARING YOUR WORKSPACE 28

CHAPTER 4: DESIGNING AND CRAFTING YOUR WOODWORKING WITH RESIN PROJECT 34
- Selecting the Right Wood 35
- Preparing the Wood 35
- Designing Your Project 36
- Choosing the Right Resin 37
- Mixing and Pouring the Resin 37
- Curing and Finishing 38

Tips and Techniques 39

CHAPTER 5: FINISHING TOUCHES AND FINISHING TECHNIQUES 42
Finishing Touches: 42
Decorative Elements 44
Finishing Techniques 46
Tips for Finishing Resin Projects 47

CHAPTER 6: TROUBLESHOOTING COMMON ISSUES WITH WOODWORKING WITH RESIN 50
Issue #1: Bubbles in the Resin 50
Issue #2: Uneven Curing 51
Issue #3: Cloudy or Yellowed Resin 52
Issue #4: Resin Sticking to the Mold 53
Issue #5: Resin Runs or Drips 54

CHAPTER 7: ADVANCED WOODWORKING WITH RESIN TECHNIQUES 56
Materials Required 56
Steps Involved: 58
Useful Tips: 60
Some Interesting Ideas Worth Exploring 61

CHAPTER 8: COMBINING RESIN WITH OTHER MATERIALS IN WOODWORKING 64
Metal 65

Glass 65
Stones 66
Fabric 66

CHAPTER 9: DIY PROJECTS USING WOODWORKING WITH RESIN 68
Resin River Coffee Table 68
Resin Wall Art 73
Resin Coasters 73
Resin and Wood Cutting Board 79
Resin and Wood Wall Clock 81
Resin Inlay Box 84
Resin Bookends 86
Resin Picture Frames 88
Resin Wall Shelf 91

CHAPTER 10: INNOVATIVE RESIN TECHNIQUES AND APPLICATIONS 94
Resin Casting with Molds 94
Creating Resin Inlays 96
Resin Lamination and Layering 99
Resin Sculpting and Carving 100
Resin Dyeing and Coloring Techniques 102

CHAPTER 11: EXPLORING SPECIALIZED RESIN PRODUCTS FOR WOODWORKING 106
Epoxy Resin for Woodworking 107
Unique Features of Epoxy Resin 107

    Steps for Using Epoxy Resin in Woodworking 107
Polyester Resin for Woodworking 109
    Unique Features of Polyester Resin: 110
    Steps for Using Polyester Resin in Woodworking. 110
UV Resin for Woodworking 111
    UV Resin Features 111
    Steps for Using UV Resin in Woodworking ... 112
Resin Adhesives and Bonding Agents 113
    Unique Features of Resin Adhesives and Bonding Agents 113
    Steps for Using Resin Adhesives and Bonding Agents: 114
Resin Fillers and Reinforcements 116
    Unique Features of Resin Fillers and Reinforcements 116
    Steps for Using Resin Fillers and Reinforcements. 116

CHAPTER 12: ADVANCED FINISHING TECHNIQUES AND SURFACE TREATMENTS 120
    High-Gloss Polishing and Buffing 121
    Matte and Satin Finishes 123
    Resin Sanding and Smoothing Techniques 125
    Resin Staining and Aging Effects 126
    Resin Surface Coatings and Protective Layers 128

CHAPTER 13: MAINTENANCE AND CARE 132
    Understanding the Characteristics of Resin 132

Tips for Maintaining and Caring for Woodworking with Resin 134

CHAPTER 14: HEALTH AND SAFETY CONSIDERATIONS IN WOODWORKING WITH RESIN 138

CHAPTER 15: INSPIRATION AND RESOURCES FOR WOODWORKING WITH RESIN 146
Inspiration 146
Resources 147
More Valuable Tips and Techniques 149
Printable PDF File of the Book 152

GLOSSARY 154

The Ultimate Guide to Woodworking with Resin

INTRODUCTION

Woodworking is an art that has been practiced for centuries, with artisans and craftsmen continuously pushing the boundaries of what can be done with wood. With the rise of new materials and techniques, woodworking has become an even more exciting and innovative field.

One of the most interesting and rapidly growing areas of woodworking is the use of resin. Resin is a versatile material that can be used to add color, texture, and depth to woodwork. It is a liquid material that hardens into a solid form, creating a stunning effect when combined with wood.

This book, "The Ultimate Guide to Woodworking with Resin" is a guide to all aspects of working with resin in woodworking projects. It covers everything from the basics of resin and woodworking, to more advanced techniques such as creating intricate designs and using different types of resin.

The book begins by introducing readers to the basics of resin, including what it is, how it works, and the different types available. It then moves on to discuss the tools and materials needed for working with resin, as well as the safety precautions that must be taken when working with this material.

Next, the book focuses on the techniques of using resin in woodworking projects. This includes creating a smooth and even surface for the resin, mixing and pouring the resin, and working with molds and forms to create specific shapes and designs.

One of the most exciting aspects of woodworking with resin is the opportunity to create stunning and unique designs. The book covers techniques such as embedding objects in resin, creating marbled effects, and using pigments and dyes to color the resin.

The guide also includes step-by-step instructions for several woodworking projects that incorporate resin. This includes creating resin river tables, adding resin to cutting boards and coasters, and using resin to create jewelry and other small items.

In addition to the practical aspects of working with resin, the book also explores the artistic and creative potential of this material. It also includes various pictures showcasing stunning resin and woodwork pieces.

Overall, "The Ultimate Guide to Woodworking with Resin" is a must-read for anyone interested in woodworking or working with resin. It offers a comprehensive guide to this exciting and innovative field, with practical advice and inspiration for both beginners and experienced woodworkers alike. Whether you're looking to create stunning resin river tables or simply add a touch of color and depth to your woodworking projects, this book has everything you need to get started.

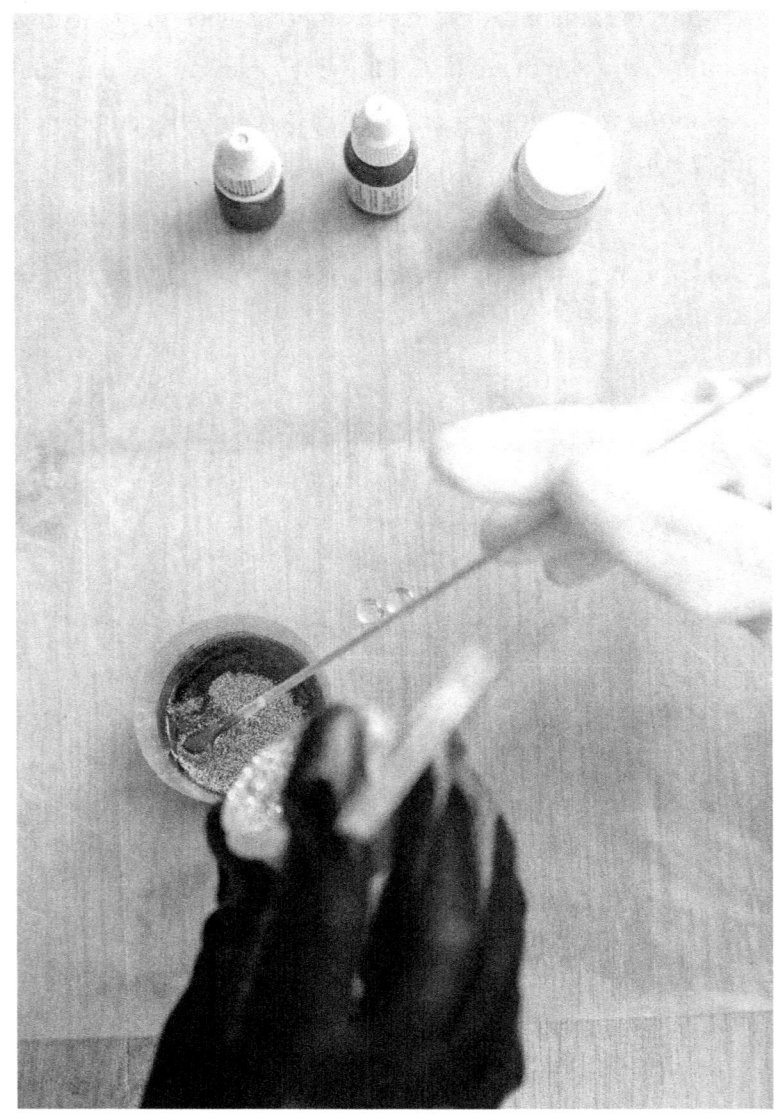

Putting Pigment in a Container with Resin

CHAPTER 1

WOODWORKING WITH RESIN

Woodworking with resin is an exciting and creative way to add a unique touch to your woodworking projects. Resin is a versatile material that can be used to fill gaps, create unique patterns, and add a glossy finish to your woodwork. With the right tools, materials, and techniques, anyone can create beautiful and durable resin-wood pieces.

In this chapter, we'll cover the basics of woodworking with resin, including the materials and tools you'll need, the types of resin available, and some popular techniques for incorporating resin into your woodworking projects.

Materials and Tools

Before you start working with resin, you'll need to gather some materials and tools. Here are the essentials:

1. **Epoxy resin:** This is the most common type of resin used in woodworking. It's a two-part system that consists of a resin and a hardener that are mixed together in equal parts. Epoxy resin is strong, durable, and easy to work with.

2. **Wood:** You'll need a piece of wood to use as the base of your project. Choose a piece that is flat and free of defects. Softwoods like pine and cedar are good choices for beginners.

3. **Mixing cups:** You'll need small mixing cups to mix your resin and hardener together.

4. **Stir sticks:** You'll need something to stir your resin and hardener together. Popsicle sticks or plastic spoons work well.

5. **Gloves:** Epoxy resin can be messy and sticky, so it's important to wear gloves to protect your hands.

6. **Heat gun/torch:** A heat gun or torch can be used to remove air bubbles from your resin once it's poured.

7. **Sandpaper:** You'll need sandpaper to sand your wood and resin once it's cured.

8. **Masking tape:** Masking tape can be used to create boundaries for your resin pour.

Torching Resin

Types of Resin

There are many different types of resin available, each with its own properties and uses. Here are the three most common types of resin used in woodworking:

a. Epoxy resin: As mentioned, this is the most common type of resin used in woodworking. It's strong, durable, and easy to work with.

b. Polyester resin: This type of resin is more brittle than epoxy resin and is not recommended for structural applications. However, it's less expensive than epoxy resin and can be used for decorative purposes.

c. Polyurethane resin: This type of resin is a good choice for outdoor projects because it's UV-resistant and doesn't yellow over time. However, it's not as strong as epoxy resin and takes longer to cure.

Resin Techniques

Now that you have your materials and tools ready, it's time to start incorporating resin into your woodworking projects. Here are some popular techniques:

1. **Filling gaps:** One of the most common uses for resin in woodworking is to fill gaps in wood. Simply mix up some epoxy resin, pour it into the gap, and use a heat gun or torch to remove any air bubbles. Once the resin has cured, sand it down to create a smooth surface.

2. **Creating unique patterns:** Resin can be used to create unique patterns in wood. To do this, pour a small amount of resin onto the wood and use a stir stick to spread it out. You can add color to your resin using pigments or dyes. Once the resin has cured, sand it down to create a smooth surface.

3. **Adding a glossy finish:** Resin can be used to add a glossy finish to wood. Simply pour a thin layer of resin over the wood and use a heat gun or torch to remove any air bubbles. Once the resin has cured, sand it down to create a smooth surface.

4. **Combining wood and resin:** One of the most popular woodworking techniques using resin is to combine wood and resin to create unique pieces. This technique involves pouring resin into a mold and then adding pieces of wood before the resin cures. This can create a stunning effect where the wood appears to be suspended in the resin.

To use this technique, you'll need a silicone mold and a piece of wood that fits inside the mold. First, coat the inside of the mold with a release agent to prevent the resin from sticking. Then, mix up some epoxy resin and pour it into the mold, filling it about a third of the way. Use a heat gun or torch to remove any air bubbles.

Next, add the piece of wood to the mold, making sure it's centered and level. Pour more resin over the wood, making sure it completely covers the wood. Use a heat gun or torch to remove any air bubbles. You can add additional layers of resin and wood to create more depth and texture.

Once the resin has cured, remove the piece from the mold and sand it down to create a smooth surface. You can then add a finish to the piece, such as a coat of polyurethane or a layer of wax.

Tips for Working with Resin

Working with resin can be a bit tricky, so here are some tips to help you get the best results:

Read the instructions carefully: Resin can be sensitive to temperature and humidity, so make sure you read the instructions carefully before you start. Some types of resin require specific temperatures and humidity levels for optimal results.

Mix thoroughly: Make sure you mix your resin and hardener thoroughly, following the instructions carefully. If the resin and hardener are not mixed properly, the resin may not cure properly.

Remove air bubbles: Use a heat gun or torch to remove any air bubbles that form in your resin. You can also use a toothpick or small brush to pop any bubbles that you see.

Use a release agent: If you're working with a mold, make sure you use a release agent to prevent the resin from sticking.

Sand carefully: Resin can be difficult to sand, so take your time and use a fine-grit sandpaper. Wear a mask to protect your lungs from the dust.

Resin-based woodworking is an exciting and imaginative way to add a unique touch to your woodworking projects. With the right materials, tools, and techniques, you can create stunning pieces that are both beautiful and durable. Whether you're filling gaps in wood, creating unique patterns, or combining wood and resin, the possibilities are endless. Just remember to read the instructions carefully, mix thoroughly, and take your time to get the best results.

A woodworker perfecting his art

CHAPTER 2

ESSENTIAL TOOLS AND MATERIALS FOR WOODWORKING WITH RESIN

Woodworking with resin has become a popular trend in recent years, and for good reason. Resin allows woodworkers to add a unique touch of creativity to their projects, and it can be used to create beautiful and functional pieces of furniture, art, and home decor. However, in order to create successful projects with resin, you need to have the right tools and materials. Here, we will be looking at the essential tools and materials you need for woodworking with resin, and I'll also provide tips and techniques to help you get started.

Resin

The first and most obvious material you need for woodworking with resin is, of course, the resin itself.

There are many types of resin available on the market, each with its own unique properties and benefits. Two of the most common types of resin used for woodworking are epoxy resin and polyester resin.

Epoxy resin is a two-part resin that is typically mixed in equal parts. It cures to a hard, clear finish and is ideal for creating a high-gloss, glass-like surface. Epoxy resin is also very strong and durable, making it ideal for use in furniture, countertops, and other high-traffic areas.

Polyester resin, on the other hand, is a single-part resin that cures to a hard, durable finish. It is less expensive than epoxy resin and is often used for smaller projects or for creating a textured, matte finish.

Both epoxy and polyester resin come in a variety of colors, so you can choose the one that best suits your project.

Mixing cups and stir sticks

When working with resin, it's important to mix it thoroughly and accurately. To do this, you'll need measuring cups and stir sticks. Mixing cups are typically made of plastic or silicone and are graduated with measurements to help you get the right ratio of resin and hardener. Stir sticks are also made of plastic or silicone and are used to mix the resin and hardener together.

It's important to use the right ratio of resin and hardener, as this will affect the curing time and strength of the finished product. Follow the manufacturer's instructions carefully and use a digital scale if necessary to ensure accurate measurements.

Heat gun or torch

To remove air bubbles from your resin, you'll need to use a heat gun or torch. Simply pass the heat gun or torch over the surface of the resin to remove any bubbles that may have formed during the mixing process.

It's important to use caution when using a heat gun or torch, as the resin can become hot and may cause burns. Always wear gloves and eye protection, and work in a well-ventilated area.

Sanding materials

After your resin has cured, you'll need to sand it to remove any rough spots or imperfections. For this, you'll need sanding materials, such as sandpaper or a sanding block. Use a coarse-grit sandpaper to remove any large bumps or rough spots, and then switch to a finer-grit sandpaper to smooth out the surface.

It's important to sand the resin carefully and evenly, as this will affect the final appearance of your project. Take your time and use a light touch to avoid scratching the surface of the resin.

Protective gear

Working with resin can be messy and potentially hazardous, so it's important to wear protective gear to keep yourself safe. Gloves, eye protection, and a respirator are essential when working with resin, as they can protect you from skin irritation, eye damage, and harmful fumes.

Choose gloves that are made of nitrile or latex, as these materials are resistant to chemicals and will protect your hands from resin and hardener. Wear safety glasses or a face shield to protect your eyes from flying debris or splashes of resin. And wear a respirator to protect your lungs from harmful fumes that can be released during the mixing and curing process.

It's important to choose the right type of respirator for the job. Look for a respirator that is rated for organic vapors, as this will protect you from the fumes that are released during the mixing and curing process. Make sure that the respirator fits properly and is comfortable to wear for extended periods of time.

Using a router for woodworking

Woodworking tools

In addition to the resin and associated materials, you'll also need a variety of woodworking tools to create your project. Here are some of the most essential tools you'll need:

1. Circular saw: A circular saw is used to make straight cuts in wood. It's essential for cutting the wood to the correct size and shape for your project.

2. Jigsaw: A jigsaw is used to make curved or angled cuts in wood. It's a versatile tool that can be used for a variety of woodworking tasks.

3. Table saw: A table saw is used to make precise cuts in wood. It's a powerful tool that can be used to cut wood to exact measurements and angles.

4. Router: A router is used to create decorative edges or shapes in wood. It can also be used to create grooves or joints in wood.

5. Drill: A drill is essential for creating holes in wood. It can be used to create holes for screws or dowels, or for creating decorative holes or patterns in wood.

6. Clamps: Clamps are essential for holding wood in place while you work on it. They come in a variety of sizes and styles, and can be used to hold pieces of wood together while glue dries, or to secure a piece of wood while you cut or shape it.

Woodworking with resin can be a fun and rewarding hobby, but it does require a bit of planning and preparation. By gathering the right tools and materials, you can create beautiful and functional pieces of furniture, art, and home decor that are sure to impress. Remember to take your time and follow the manufacturer's instructions carefully, and always wear protective gear to keep yourself safe. With a little practice and patience, you can create stunning works of art that showcase your creativity and skill.

Drilling

CHAPTER 3

PREPARING YOUR WORKSPACE

Woodworking with resin can be an incredibly rewarding and exciting experience. The combination of natural wood and the synthetic material of resin can create beautiful and unique pieces that are both functional and decorative. However, in order to ensure the best results possible, it is important to properly prepare your workspace. In this chapter, we will go over some practical tips and techniques for preparing your workspace for woodworking with resin.

Choose the Right Space

The first step in preparing your workspace for woodworking with resin is to choose the right space. Ideally, this space should be well-ventilated and have plenty of natural light. It should also be a space that is easy to clean and keep free of dust and debris. If you don't have a dedicated workshop, consider using a garage or outdoor space, weather permitting.

Set Up a Dust Collection System

Dust can be a major problem when working with resin, as it can interfere with the resin's ability to bond properly with the wood. In order to minimize dust and debris in your workspace, consider setting up a dust collection system. This can be as simple as using a shop vac or dust extractor with a fine dust filter, or as complex as installing a dedicated dust collection system with ducting and a cyclone separator.

Create a Clean Work Surface

In addition to minimizing dust and debris, it is important to create a clean work surface for woodworking with resin. This means wiping down your workspace with a damp cloth to remove any dust or debris, and then covering it with a layer of plastic or wax paper. This will not only help to prevent dust from settling on your workpiece, but will also make it easier to clean up any spills or drips.

Protect Your Tools and Equipment

Resin can be incredibly sticky and difficult to remove once it has dried. To prevent your tools and equipment from becoming coated in resin, cover them with masking tape or wax paper. This includes not just your woodworking tools, but also your measuring and mixing tools, such as measuring cups, mixing sticks, and syringes.

Use a Resin-Specific Mixing Container

When mixing resin, it is important to use a container that is specifically designed for resin. This is because many plastics and other materials can react with resin, causing it to cure too quickly or not bond properly with the wood. Look for containers that are made from polypropylene or polyethylene, as these materials are resistant to resin.

Keep Your Resin and Hardener Separate

Resin and hardener should always be kept separate until it is time to mix them together. This is because resin and hardener can react with each other even before they are mixed, leading to a premature cure. Store your resin and hardener in separate containers and mix them together only when you are ready to start working.

Use a Digital Scale for Precise Measurements

When working with resin, it is important to measure accurately in order to achieve the desired result. This means using a digital scale to measure both resin and hardener. Digital scales are more precise than measuring cups or syringes, and can help you achieve consistent results.

Work in Small Batches

Resin has a limited working time, which means that it will start to cure and harden as soon as it is mixed with hardener. To prevent your resin from curing before you are ready, work in small batches. This will allow you to mix and apply the resin before it starts to cure, and will also give you more control over the process.

Use a Heat Gun to Remove Air Bubbles

Air bubbles can be a common problem when working with resin. To remove air bubbles from your workpiece, use a heat gun or a propane torch. Hold the heat gun a few inches away from the surface of the resin and move it back and forth in a sweeping motion. This will help to release any trapped air bubbles and give you a smooth and even finish.

Wear Personal Protective Equipment

Working with resin can be hazardous if proper safety precautions are not taken. It is important to wear personal protective equipment, such as gloves, safety glasses, and a respirator, to protect yourself from the fumes and chemicals in the resin. Always follow the manufacturer's instructions for safe use and disposal of the resin.

Allow Proper Curing Time

Resin requires a certain amount of time to cure and harden properly. This can vary depending on the type of resin and the temperature and humidity of your workspace. Be sure to allow adequate curing time before handling or sanding your workpiece. It is also important to follow the manufacturer's instructions for proper curing time and temperature.

Clean Up Properly

After you have finished working with resin, it is important to clean up properly. This includes wiping down your workspace with a damp cloth to remove any resin or dust, and disposing of any leftover resin and hardener according to the manufacturer's instructions. You should also clean your tools and equipment thoroughly with isopropyl alcohol or acetone to remove any resin residue.

Obviously speaking, woodworking with resin can be a pretty creative process, but it requires careful preparation and attention to detail. By choosing the right workspace, using the proper tools and equipment, and following safety protocols, you can achieve beautiful and unique results. So go ahead, get creative, and enjoy the process of woodworking with resin!

CHAPTER 4

DESIGNING AND CRAFTING YOUR WOODWORKING WITH RESIN PROJECT

Woodworking projects are always fun and exciting to undertake, especially when you get to incorporate unique and creative elements like resin. Resin is a versatile material that can be used to create stunning designs and add depth and dimension to your woodworking projects. Whether you are a seasoned woodworker or a beginner, incorporating resin into your woodworking projects can take your skills and craftsmanship to the next level.

In this guide, we will explore the process of designing and crafting a woodworking project with resin. We'll cover everything from selecting the right type of wood to choosing the appropriate type of resin for your project. So, let's get started!

Selecting the Right Wood

The first step in designing and crafting a woodworking project with resin is to select the right type of wood. Not all woods are suitable for use with resin, so it's important to choose a type of wood that is strong enough to withstand the pressure of the resin and will also complement the resin's visual appeal.

Some of the best woods for resin projects include maple, walnut, and oak. These woods are strong and durable, making them ideal for projects that require a lot of sanding and shaping. Other popular woods for resin projects include cherry, ash, and birch.

When selecting your wood, look for pieces that are free of knots, cracks, and other imperfections. You want a piece of wood that is smooth and uniform in texture, as this will make it easier to work with and create a beautiful finished product.

Preparing the Wood

Once you have selected your wood, it's time to prepare it for the resin. The first step is to sand the wood down to a smooth surface. Use a coarse grit sandpaper to remove any rough spots or imperfections, then gradually work your way up to a finer grit sandpaper until the surface is completely smooth.

After sanding, wipe the surface of the wood with a clean cloth to remove any dust or debris. This is important because any particles left on the surface can affect the adhesion of the resin.

Designing Your Project

With your wood prepped and ready to go, it's time to start thinking about the design of your project. This is where you can let your creativity run wild and come up with a unique and eye-catching design that incorporates the resin.

One popular design technique is to create a river or ocean effect using resin. This involves pouring the resin into a groove or channel cut into the wood, which creates the illusion of water flowing through the piece. You can also use resin to fill in cracks or knots in the wood, which can create interesting visual effects.

Other design ideas include creating abstract patterns or designs, embedding objects like rocks or shells into the resin, or using different colors of resin to create a multi-dimensional effect.

Choosing the Right Resin

Now that you have a design in mind, it's time to choose the right type of resin for your project. There are two main types of resin: epoxy resin and polyester resin.

Epoxy resin is the most popular type of resin for woodworking projects. It is a clear, high-gloss resin that is easy to work with and creates a durable, long-lasting finish. It is also resistant to heat, chemicals, and UV rays, making it ideal for projects that will be exposed to the elements.

Polyester resin is another option, but it is less commonly used in woodworking projects. It is a clear, low-viscosity resin that is easy to mix and pour, but it is not as durable as epoxy resin and can yellow over time.

Mixing and Pouring the Resin

Once you have selected your resin, it's time to mix and pour it onto your wood. The mixing and pouring process is critical to the success of your project, so it's important to follow the manufacturer's instructions carefully.

First, you need to prepare your workspace by laying down a drop cloth or newspaper to protect your work surface.

You should also wear gloves and a respirator mask to protect yourself from the fumes.

To mix the resin, follow the instructions on the package. Typically, you will need to mix equal parts resin and hardener together in a mixing cup. Use a stir stick to mix the two components together thoroughly for several minutes.

Once the resin is mixed, pour it onto the wood in the desired areas. Use a spreader or a brush to spread the resin evenly across the surface of the wood. If you are creating a river or ocean effect, use a groove or channel to guide the resin into the desired shape.

If you are embedding objects into the resin, place them into the resin while it is still wet. You can also add pigment or dye to the resin to create different colors or effects.

Curing and Finishing

After pouring the resin, it's time to let it cure. The curing time will vary depending on the type of resin you are using and the temperature and humidity of your workspace. Follow the manufacturer's instructions for curing times and conditions.

Once the resin is cured, you can begin finishing your project. Use a fine grit sandpaper to sand down any rough spots or edges on the wood or resin. You can also use a buffing wheel or polish to bring out the shine of the resin.

If you want to add an extra layer of protection to your project, you can apply a clear coat of polyurethane or lacquer. This will help protect the wood and resin from scratches and damage.

Tips and Techniques

Here are a few tips and techniques to keep in mind when designing and crafting your woodworking project with resin:

- Practice on scrap wood first to get a feel for working with resin and to test out different design ideas.

- Use a heat gun or torch to remove any bubbles that form in the resin as it cures.

- Use a release agent, such as petroleum jelly or silicone spray, on any surfaces you don't want the resin to stick to.

- Experiment with different colors and effects by adding pigment, dye, or other materials to the resin.

- Don't rush the curing process. Be patient and give the resin enough time to fully cure before finishing your project.

Designing and crafting a woodworking project with resin helps to take your woodworking skills to the next level. Whether you're creating a river effect or embedding objects into the resin, there are endless design possibilities to explore.

By following the steps outlined in this guide and keeping a few tips and techniques in mind, you can create a beautiful and unique woodworking project that showcases your craftsmanship and creativity. So, get out there and start experimenting with resin in your woodworking projects!

A resin painting

CHAPTER 5

FINISHING TOUCHES AND FINISHING TECHNIQUES

Once again, welcome to the exciting world of woodworking with resin! In this chapter, we will discuss the importance of finishing touches and finishing techniques in your resin woodworking projects. As a beginner or a seasoned woodworker, mastering these techniques will help you achieve a polished and professional look for your projects.

Finishing Touches

The finishing touches are the final steps that you take to complete your resin woodworking project. These steps are essential to ensure that your project looks its best and has a durable finish. The finishing touches include sanding, applying a protective finish, and adding any decorative elements.

1. Sanding:

Sanding is a critical step in the finishing process. It helps to remove any rough spots, scratches, or imperfections in the wood and resin. Sanding also creates a smooth surface that is ready to accept a protective finish. You should start with a coarse-grit sandpaper, such as 80 or 100 grit, to remove any rough spots. Then, move up to a finer grit, such as 220 or 320 grit, to smooth out the surface. Finally, use a very fine grit, such as 400 or 600 grit, to create a smooth finish.

2. Protective Finish:

Once you have sanded the surface, it's time to apply a protective finish. This finish will protect the wood and resin from moisture, UV rays, and other environmental factors that can cause damage. There are many different types of protective finishes available, including oils, waxes, and varnishes.

3. Oils:

Oils are an excellent choice for protecting and enhancing the natural beauty of the wood. They penetrate the wood fibers and provide a deep, rich finish. Some popular oils include tung oil, linseed oil, and teak oil. When using oil, be sure to apply it evenly and let it dry thoroughly before handling the project.

4. Waxes:

Waxes are another option for protecting the wood and resin. They provide a hard, durable finish that is resistant to scratches and abrasions. Some popular waxes include beeswax, carnauba wax, and paraffin wax. When using wax, apply it evenly and buff the surface with a soft cloth to create a smooth finish.

5. Varnishes:

Varnishes are a popular choice for protecting and adding a glossy finish to the wood and resin. They are available in different sheens, from matte to high-gloss. Some popular varnishes include polyurethane, lacquer, and shellac. When using varnish, be sure to apply it evenly and let it dry thoroughly before handling the project.

Decorative Elements

Once you have applied the protective finish, you can add decorative elements to your project. This is an excellent opportunity to personalize your work and add some unique touches. Some popular decorative elements include inlay, carving, and painting.

Inlay:

Inlay is a decorative technique that involves embedding small pieces of material, such as metal, wood, or stone, into the surface of the wood and resin. Inlay can create intricate patterns and designs that add a beautiful touch to your project. Some popular inlay materials include mother-of-pearl, abalone, and brass.

Carving:

Carving is another decorative technique that involves removing small pieces of wood to create intricate designs and patterns. Carving can add depth and texture to your project and is an excellent way to showcase your woodworking skills.

Painting:

Painting is a great way to add color and personality to your project. You can use acrylic or oil paints to create unique designs and patterns on the surface of the wood and resin. Be sure to use a primer before painting to ensure that the paint adheres properly to the surface.

Finishing Techniques

Finishing techniques are the methods that you use to apply the protective finish to your project. There are several different techniques that you can use to apply the protective finish, including brushing, spraying, and wiping.

Brushing

Brushing is a popular technique for applying the protective finish. It is a simple method that involves using a brush to apply the finish in even strokes. When brushing, be sure to use a high-quality brush that is designed for the type of finish that you are using. You should also apply the finish in thin, even coats, and be sure to brush in the direction of the wood grain.

Spraying

Spraying is another popular technique for applying the protective finish. It is a fast and efficient method that creates a smooth, even finish. You can use a spray gun or a can of spray finish to apply the protective coating. When spraying, be sure to wear a mask to protect your lungs, and apply the finish in a well-ventilated area.

Wiping

Wiping is a technique that involves applying the protective finish with a cloth. This method is ideal for small projects or for touch-ups. To use this technique, simply apply a small amount of finish to a clean, soft cloth, and wipe it onto the surface in thin, even coats.

Tips for Finishing Resin Projects

Here are some tips that will help you achieve the best results when finishing your resin woodworking projects:

- Sand the surface of the resin before applying the protective finish. This will help the finish adhere better to the surface and create a smoother finish.

- Be sure to apply the protective finish in a well-ventilated area. Some finishes can release fumes that can be harmful if inhaled.

- Use a clean, high-quality brush or spray gun to apply the protective finish. This will help to create an even finish and avoid brush strokes or drips.

- Let each coat of finish dry thoroughly before applying the next coat. This will help to ensure that the finish adheres properly and creates a durable surface.

- Be patient and take your time. Finishing a project can take time, but the results are worth it.

Finishing touches and finishing techniques are essential components of woodworking with resin. By mastering these techniques, you can create beautiful and durable projects that showcase your woodworking skills. Remember to sand the surface, apply a protective finish, and add decorative elements to create a personalized project. These tips will help you achieve a polished and professional look for your resin woodworking projects, irrespective of your current level as a woodworker.

A woodworker on a project

CHAPTER 6

TROUBLESHOOTING COMMON ISSUES WITH WOODWORKING WITH RESIN

Woodworking with resin has become increasingly popular in recent years, with many people using this versatile material to create stunning and unique pieces of art and furniture. However, as with any craft, there are common issues that can arise when working with resin that can be frustrating and time-consuming to resolve. In this section, we will explore some of the most common issues with woodworking with resin and provide practical tips to troubleshoot these problems.

Issue #1: Bubbles in the Resin

One of the most common issues with woodworking with resin is the presence of bubbles in the final product. Bubbles can occur during the mixing process, when the resin is poured, or even during the curing process. Bubbles can be unsightly and can ruin the overall appearance of the finished piece.

Solution: Preventing bubbles in the resin requires careful attention to detail during the mixing and pouring process. First, make sure that the mixing container is clean and free of any debris. Next, stir the resin slowly and steadily, being careful not to introduce too much air into the mixture. When pouring the resin, try to pour it in a thin stream to avoid trapping air bubbles. Finally, if bubbles do appear in the resin, they can often be removed by using a heat gun or torch to carefully heat the surface of the resin, which will cause the bubbles to rise to the surface and pop.

Additional Tip: Try pouring a small amount of resin into a mixing container and stirring it vigorously to see how many bubbles form. Then, try stirring the resin slowly and steadily to see if this reduces the number of bubbles.

Issue #2: Uneven Curing

Another common issue with woodworking with resin is uneven curing. This can result in areas of the finished piece being softer or tackier than others, or even areas that remain sticky or uncured.

Solution: Uneven curing can often be avoided by following the manufacturer's instructions for mixing and curing the resin. It is important to use the correct ratio of resin and hardener, and to mix the two components thoroughly. When pouring the resin, make sure that it is evenly distributed and that there are no areas that are thicker or thinner than others. If uneven curing does occur, it may be necessary to sand down the affected area and reapply a new layer of resin.

Additional Tip: Try pouring a small amount of resin onto a flat surface and spreading it out to see if it cures evenly. You can also try pouring resin into a mold and checking for any areas that do not cure properly.

Issue #3: Cloudy or Yellowed Resin

Another issue that can occur with woodworking with resin is that the resin can become cloudy or yellowed over time. This can be caused by a variety of factors, including exposure to UV light, improper mixing, or using the wrong type of resin.

Solution: To avoid cloudy or yellowed resin, it is important to use a high-quality resin that is designed for the specific project you are working on. Make sure that you mix the resin and hardener thoroughly and according to the manufacturer's instructions. When pouring the resin, avoid exposing it to UV light, which can cause discoloration. If you are working on a project that will be exposed to sunlight, consider using a UV-resistant resin or applying a UV-resistant coating after the resin has cured.

Added Tip: Try pouring a small amount of resin into a clear container and exposing it to sunlight for a few hours to see if it becomes cloudy or yellowed. You can also try mixing the resin and hardener together and seeing if the mixture becomes cloudy or discolored.

Issue #4: Resin Sticking to the Mold

One of the most frustrating issues with woodworking with resin is when the resin sticks to the mold, making it difficult or impossible to remove the finished product from the mold without damaging it.

Solution: To avoid resin sticking to the mold, it is important to properly prepare the mold before pouring the resin. This can be done by applying a release agent, such as mold release spray or wax, to the mold. It is also important to ensure that the mold is completely clean and dry before pouring the resin. If the resin does stick to the mold, try freezing the mold for a few hours, which can help to loosen the resin and make it easier to remove.

Additional Tip: Try pouring resin into a mold without using a release agent to see how difficult it is to remove the finished product. Then, try using a release agent and see if this makes it easier to remove the finished product without damaging the mold.

Issue #5: Resin Runs or Drips

Another issue that can occur when working with resin is that it can run or drip, creating uneven or unsightly areas on the finished product.

Solution: To avoid resin runs or drips, it is important to use a thick enough layer of resin that it will not run or drip. This can be done by pouring the resin in thin layers and allowing each layer to cure before adding another layer. It is also important to use a level surface when pouring the resin to ensure that it does not pool or run to one side.

Additional Tip: Try pouring resin onto a surface that is not level to see how it runs and drips. Then, try pouring resin onto a level surface and see how it spreads evenly.

Always bear this in mind that woodworking with resin can be a rewarding and creative process, but it is important to be aware of the common issues that can arise when working with this material. By following the tips and techniques outlined in this chapter, you can avoid these issues and create beautiful, high-quality pieces of art and furniture. Remember to always read and follow the manufacturer's instructions for the resin you are using, and don't be afraid to experiment and try new techniques to create unique and stunning works of art.

CHAPTER 7

ADVANCED WOODWORKING WITH RESIN TECHNIQUES

Woodworking with resin is a popular and exciting technique that has been around for many years. It is an innovative and creative way of adding color, texture, and depth to woodwork. Here, we will look at advanced woodworking with resin techniques and explore how to make resin a part of your woodworking projects. We will discuss the materials required, the steps involved, and some useful tips to make your woodworking projects more engaging, practical, and interactive.

Materials Required

To get started with woodworking with resin, you will need the following materials:

Wood: The first and foremost requirement for woodworking with resin is wood. Any type of wood can be used for this purpose, but the more natural-looking and textured the wood is, the better the result will be. Hardwoods like maple, oak, and walnut are great options for woodworking projects.

Resin: There are two types of resin that can be used for woodworking projects: epoxy and polyester resin. Epoxy resin is more commonly used in woodworking projects due to its durability, strength, and versatility. Polyester resin is also used, but it is not as strong as epoxy and is prone to cracking and yellowing over time.

Pigments and Dyes: Pigments and dyes are used to add color to the resin. These can be purchased in various colors and can be mixed to create custom colors.

Mixing Containers: Mixing containers are used to mix the resin and hardener. These can be plastic cups or any other container that is disposable.

Mixing Sticks: Mixing sticks are used to mix the resin and hardener. These can be popsicle sticks, wooden dowels, or any other tool that is disposable.

Heat Gun: A heat gun is used to remove any bubbles that may form in the resin. This is an important step as it ensures that the resin is evenly distributed and that there are no air pockets.

Sandpaper: Sandpaper is used to sand the wood after the resin has cured. This is an important step as it ensures that the wood is smooth and even.

Safety Equipment: Safety equipment like gloves, goggles, and a respirator should be worn while working with resin. This is important as resin can be toxic and can cause skin irritation.

Steps Involved:

1. **Prepare the Wood:** The first step in woodworking with resin is to prepare the wood. This involves sanding the wood to ensure that it is smooth and even. It is important to ensure that the wood is free from any dust, debris, or oils.

2. **Seal the Wood:** Once the wood is sanded, it should be sealed. This can be done using a wood sealer or a clear coat of epoxy resin. This step is important as it ensures that the resin adheres well to the wood.

3. **Mix the Resin:** The resin and hardener should be mixed according to the instructions on the package. It is important to ensure that the resin and hardener are mixed in the correct ratio, as this affects the curing time and strength of the resin.

4. **Add Pigments and Dyes:** Once the resin is mixed, pigments and dyes can be added. These should be mixed well to ensure that the color is evenly distributed.

5. **Pour the Resin:** The resin should be poured onto the wood. It is important to ensure that the resin is evenly distributed and that there are no air pockets.

6. **Remove Bubbles:** A heat gun should be used to remove any bubbles that may form in the resin. This is an important step as it ensures that the resin is evenly distributed and that there are no air pockets.

7. **Allow to Cure:** The resin should be allowed to cure according to the instructions on the package. This can take anywhere from a few hours to several days, depending on the type of resin used.

8. **Sand the Resin:** Once the resin has cured, the wood can be sanded to remove any rough edges or imperfections. It is important to use a fine-grit sandpaper to ensure that the surface is smooth and even.

9. **Apply a Finish:** A finish can be applied to the wood to protect the surface and enhance its appearance. This can be done using a clear coat of epoxy resin, a wood stain, or any other type of finish that suits the project.

Useful Tips:

Practice Safety: Always wear safety equipment when working with resin. This includes gloves, goggles, and a respirator.

Choose the Right Wood: Hardwoods like maple, oak, and walnut are great options for woodworking projects with resin. Make sure that the wood is free from any dust, debris, or oils before applying the resin.

Mix the Resin Correctly: Follow the instructions on the package to ensure that the resin and hardener are mixed in the correct ratio. This affects the curing time and strength of the resin.

Use Pigments and Dyes Sparingly: Start with small amounts of pigment or dye and gradually add more as needed. This allows for greater control over the color and ensures that the resin does not become too thick.

Remove Bubbles: Use a heat gun to remove any bubbles that may form in the resin. This ensures that the resin is evenly distributed and that there are no air pockets.

Allow the Resin to Cure Completely: It is important to allow the resin to cure completely before sanding or applying a finish. This ensures that the resin is strong and durable.

Experiment with Different Techniques: There are many different techniques that can be used with woodworking and resin. Try different techniques to create unique and creative projects.

Some Interesting Ideas Worth Exploring

1. <u>Host a Workshop:</u> Host a workshop to teach others about woodworking with resin. This can be a fun and interactive way to share knowledge and creativity with others. By teaching others, you will have a better understanding of the "trade".

2. <u>Collaborate with Other Woodworkers:</u> Collaborate with other woodworkers to create unique and creative projects. This allows for greater creativity and can result in stunning pieces of art.

3. <u>Share Your Work:</u> Share your work on social media or online forums to get feedback and inspiration from others. This can also help to build a community of like-minded individuals who share a passion for woodworking with resin.

4. <u>Participate in Competitions:</u> Participate in woodworking competitions to showcase your skills and creativity. This can be a fun and challenging way to push yourself and improve your craft.

Woodworking with resin is a fascinating and creative way to add color, texture, and depth to woodwork. By following the steps outlined in this chapter using the right materials, you can create stunning pieces of art that are both functional and beautiful. Whether you are a beginner or an experienced woodworker, there are many techniques and ideas to explore with woodworking and resin. With a little practice, you can create unique and creative projects that showcase your skills and passion for woodworking.

Resin-based woodwork

CHAPTER 8

COMBINING RESIN WITH OTHER MATERIALS IN WOODWORKING

Resin has become a popular material in woodworking, and for good reason. It's a versatile material that can be used to create a variety of beautiful and functional pieces. While it's commonly used to create unique and eye-catching finishes on wood, resin can also be combined with other materials to create stunning and practical pieces.

Combining resin with other materials can add depth, texture, and visual interest to your projects. From metal to glass to stones, resin can be used to create unique and beautiful pieces that are both engaging and practical.

In this guide, we'll explore some of the most popular materials that can be combined with resin in woodworking, and share some tips for working with this versatile material.

Metal

Combining resin with metal can create a beautiful and durable finish that can be used in a variety of applications. One popular way to use resin with metal is to create a unique tabletop. By pouring resin over metal sheeting, you can create a smooth and durable surface that's both visually stunning and practical.

Another way to combine resin with metal is to create jewelry. By embedding metal pieces into the resin, you can create beautiful and unique pieces that are sure to turn heads. You can also use resin to create a protective finish on metal, helping to prevent rust and corrosion.

Glass

Glass is another material that can be combined with resin to create beautiful and unique pieces. One popular application is to create resin-filled vases or bowls. By pouring resin into a glass vessel, you can create a beautiful and durable finish that's both functional and visually stunning.

Another way to use resin with glass is to create beautiful and unique pendants or other jewelry pieces. By embedding glass pieces into the resin, you can create beautiful and unique pieces that are sure to be conversation starters.

Stones

Stones are another popular material that can be combined with resin to create beautiful and unique pieces. One popular way to use resin with stones is to create a resin-filled countertop. By embedding stones into the resin, you can create a beautiful and durable surface that's both functional and visually stunning.

Another way to use resin with stones is to create beautiful and unique pendants or other jewelry pieces. By embedding stones into the resin, you can create beautiful and unique pieces that are sure to be conversation starters.

Fabric

Combining resin with fabric can create a stiff and durable finish that can be used in a variety of applications. One popular way to use resin with fabric is to create unique and durable coasters. By dipping fabric into the resin and allowing it to dry, you can create a stiff and durable finish that's both practical and visually stunning.

Another way to use resin with fabric is to create beautiful and unique pendants or other jewelry pieces. By embedding fabric into the resin, you can create beautiful and unique pieces that are sure to be conversation starters.

Combining resin with other materials can add depth, texture, and visual interest to your projects.

CHAPTER 9

DIY PROJECTS USING WOODWORKING WITH RESIN

Woodworking with resin has become an increasingly popular trend in the world of DIY projects. This combination of materials allows for a variety of creative possibilities and can result in stunning pieces that are both beautiful and functional.

In this chapter, we will explore some practical and engaging DIY projects using woodworking with resin that you can try at home.

Resin River Coffee Table

A resin river coffee table is a stunning piece that will be the centerpiece of any living room. The process involves pouring resin into a river-like groove cut into the wood, which gives the illusion of a flowing river in the center of the table.

To create a resin river coffee table, you will need:

1. **Wood Slab:** Choose a hardwood with character. Look for slabs with contrasting grain patterns, knots, or spalting (natural wood decay patterns) for a more dramatic effect. Maple, walnut, elm, and oak are popular choices. Ensure the slab is dry and properly acclimatized to your workshop environment to prevent warping later. Thickness should be around 1.5-2 inches for stability.

2. **Resin:** Opt for high-quality, crystal-clear epoxy resin specifically formulated for woodworking applications. These resins offer superior clarity, self-leveling properties, and better adhesion to wood.

3. **Pigment (Optional):** For a colored river effect, choose pigments compatible with epoxy resin. Test the pigment in a small batch first to ensure desired color and translucency.

Tools of the Trade:

Router: A plunge router with a variable speed control is ideal. Invest in a solid carbide bit specifically designed for epoxy routing. Choose a bit size that complements the desired width of your river.

Safety Gear: Wear safety glasses, a dust mask, and hearing protection while routing and sanding.

Clamps and Supports: You'll need a variety of clamps to secure the wood slab during routing and finishing. Sturdy sawhorses or a workbench with a flat surface are essential for supporting the table throughout the build.

Step-by-Step Direction:

1. **Prepare the Wood Slab:** Plane the slab perfectly flat to ensure the resin sits level. Sand the entire surface to a smooth finish (around 120 grit sandpaper). Trace the outline of your desired table shape onto the slab and cut with a circular saw or jigsaw, leaving a clean edge.

2. **Routing the River Path:** Clamp the slab securely to your work surface. Set the router depth to slightly more than half the thickness of your slab. Make multiple passes with the router, starting from the center and working outwards, to achieve the desired river channel profile. Use a template or freehand routing for a more organic river shape. Clean out any router dust with compressed air.

3. **Fine-Tuning the Channel:** After routing, meticulously clean the channel with a tack cloth to remove all dust particles that could cause imperfections in the resin. Use a chisel or sanding drum attachment on your rotary tool to refine the edges of the channel for a crisp look.

4. **Resin Mixing and Pouring:** Work in a well-ventilated area with a respirator. Precise resin-to-hardener ratio is crucial, so follow the manufacturer's instructions meticulously. Once mixed, pour a small amount of resin into the channel to coat the bottom and sides. Tilt the slab to ensure complete coverage and eliminate air bubbles. Use a heat gun held at a safe distance to gently pop any bubbles that surface.

5. **Layered Pouring (Optional):** For a more dynamic river effect, consider pouring the resin in layers with different colors or even embed small objects like pebbles or dried flowers between pours. Allow each layer to cure partially before adding the next for best results.

6. **Leveling and Curing:** Once the channel is filled, use a level to ensure the resin sits flat. A strategically placed artist's palette knife can help nudge the resin for a perfect finish. Cover the table to prevent dust from settling on the curing resin. Curing time varies depending on the resin brand; refer to the manufacturer's specifications.

7. **Sanding and Finishing:** Once cured, the resin might have a slight inlay compared to the wood. Use a sanding block to gradually flatten the surface, starting with coarse grit sandpaper (around 80 grit) and progressing to finer grits (120-220 grit) for a polished finish. Wipe away dust with a damp cloth.

8. **Wood Finishing:** Apply your preferred wood finish to the entire table surface, following the product's application instructions. Oil or varnish are popular choices, depending on the desired sheen and level of protection.

More Tips:

- **Practice Routing:** Before tackling your main slab, practice routing techniques on scrap wood to ensure clean cuts and comfortable control of the router.
- **Pigment Dispersion:** Thoroughly mix pigment into the resin to avoid streaks. Test your mix on a separate surface to ensure even color distribution.
- **Temperature Control:** Maintain a warm shop environment (around 70°F) for optimal resin cure time and flow.
- **Flood Coat the Entire Surface (Optional):** For a flawless, even finish, consider pouring a thin layer of

clear resin over the entire table surface after the river has cured and been sanded.

A resin coffee table

Resin Wall Art

Resin wall art is a unique and eye-catching addition to any room in your home. The process involves pouring resin onto a wooden surface and manipulating it to create interesting patterns and textures.

Material Selection:

Wooden Canvas: Select high-quality wood with a flat, stable surface. Pre-made wood panels are readily available, but adventurous crafters can construct their own canvas from birch plywood. Opt for a thickness between ½ inch to ¾ inch for sturdiness.

Resin: Choose crystal-clear epoxy resin formulated for artistic applications. This ensures clarity, self-leveling properties, and optimal adhesion. Consider UV-resistant resin if your art will receive direct sunlight to prevent yellowing over time.

Pigments (Optional): Explore a world of color with pigments compatible with epoxy resin. Popular choices include powdered pigments, mica powders, and alcohol inks. Experiment on a small test piece to determine color vibrancy and desired translucency within the resin.

Mold-Making Materials (Optional): For creating specific shapes or 3D effects, consider using silicone molds or building custom molds with MDF (medium-density fiberboard) and a sealant.

Crafting Your Masterpiece:

1. **Surface Preparation:** Meticulously sand the wooden canvas with 120 grit sandpaper to achieve a smooth, even texture. Wipe away any sanding dust with a tack cloth to ensure a perfect bond between the wood and resin.

2. **Planning Your Design (Optional):** Sketch or digitally design your desired artwork beforehand. This can be especially helpful for incorporating specific shapes, color palettes, or cell effects (creating organic, cloud-like formations within the resin).

3. **Resin Mixing:** Work in a clean, dust-free environment. Precise resin-to-hardener ratios are crucial, so meticulously follow the manufacturer's instructions. Mix thoroughly using a designated stirring utensil to ensure even distribution and avoid pockets of unmixed resin that can affect curing.

4. **Color Infusion (Optional):** For a vibrant art piece, introduce pigments into a portion of your mixed resin. Maintain a separate container of clear resin for contrasting effects or layering techniques.

Pouring Techniques:

Single pour: For a simple yet elegant look, pour the mixed resin directly onto the prepared wooden canvas. Tilt the canvas to achieve an even spread, allowing the resin to reach all edges.

Layered pour: To create depth and visual intrigue, pour the resin in multiple layers with contrasting colors or even embed small objects like dried flowers, coffee grounds, or metallic flakes between pours. Allow each layer to partially cure before adding the next to prevent unwanted mixing.

Mold application: If using molds, pour the mixed resin into the prepared mold, ensuring complete coverage and eliminating air bubbles with a gentle tap or a heat gun. Let the resin cure partially within the mold before carefully demolding it onto the wooden canvas for a dimensional effect.

Resin Manipulation: This is where your artistic expression comes alive! While the resin is still in its liquid state, use tools like palette knives, straws, or combs to gently manipulate the resin and create swirls, streaks, or patterns. The heat gun becomes your friend here – use it strategically to move the resin, pop air bubbles, and promote cell formation.

Curing and Finishing: Once you're satisfied with your creation, cover the artwork loosely to prevent dust from settling but allow for proper ventilation. Curing time varies depending on the resin brand and thickness, so refer to the manufacturer's specifications.

Sanding and Touch-Ups (Optional): Once cured, the resin surface might have slight imperfections. Use a sanding block with fine-grit sandpaper (around 220 grit) to achieve a perfectly smooth finish. You can even buff the surface with a microfiber cloth for an extra touch of shine.

Framing (Optional): While not necessary for all resin art pieces, a well-chosen frame can enhance your artwork and complement your décor.

More Tips:

- **Always wear gloves and safety glasses** when handling resin. Opt for nitrile gloves with good chemical resistance. Fumes can occur during mixing, so ensure proper ventilation by working in a well-ventilated space or wearing a respirator if necessary.
- **Practice pouring techniques** on a disposable surface like a silicone sheet before tackling your final piece.
- **Work in small batches**, especially when experimenting with colors or techniques, to avoid wasting resin due to mistakes.
- **Maintain a clean work area** to prevent dust or debris from contaminating your resin art.
- **Don't be afraid to experiment!** The beauty of resin art lies in its versatility. Embrace the flow of the resin and create art that reflects your unique style.

Resin Coasters

Resin coasters are a practical and fun DIY project that can be customized to fit any style or decor. The process involves pouring resin into a mold and adding embellishments such as glitter or dried flowers.

To create resin coasters, you will need:

- Resin
- Pigment (optional)
- Coaster molds (can be purchased or made from silicone)
- Embellishments (such as glitter or dried flowers)
- A mixing cup and stirring utensil
- Sandpaper

Mix the resin according to the manufacturer's instructions, adding pigment if desired. Pour the resin into the coaster molds, taking care not to overflow. Add embellishments such as glitter or dried flowers to the resin.

Allow the resin to cure for the recommended amount of time, typically 24 to 48 hours. Once cured, remove the coasters from the molds and sand the surface of the resin until it is smooth and level. Finish the coasters with a cork backing to prevent them from scratching surfaces, and your resin coasters are complete!

A resin coaster

Resin and Wood Cutting Board

A resin and wood cutting board is a functional and beautiful addition to any kitchen. The process involves pouring resin into a wooden mold and adding wooden strips to create a unique pattern.

To create a resin and wood cutting board, you will need:

- A wooden mold (can be made from plywood)
- Resin
- Pigment (optional)
- Wooden strips (can be purchased or cut from scrap wood)
- A mixing cup and stirring utensil
- Sandpaper
- A saw

Start by cutting the wooden strips to the desired length and width. Arrange the strips in a pattern that you like, leaving a small gap between each strip. Place the wooden mold around the wooden strips, making sure it is level.

Mix the resin according to the manufacturer's instructions, adding pigment if desired. Pour the resin into the mold, making sure it covers the wooden strips completely. Use a torch or heat gun to remove any air bubbles that may have formed.

Allow the resin to cure for the recommended amount of time, typically 24 to 48 hours. Once cured, remove the cutting board from the mold and sand the surface of the resin until it is smooth and level with the wooden strips. Finish the cutting board with food-grade mineral oil to protect it from water damage and your resin and wood cutting board is complete!

Resin and wood cutting board

Resin and Wood Wall Clock

A resin and wood wall clock is a functional and unique piece of home decor that can be customized to fit any style or decor. The process involves pouring resin into a wooden mold and adding a clock mechanism.

To create a resin and wood wall clock, you will need:

A wooden mold (can be made from plywood)

- Resin
- Pigment (optional)
- A clock mechanism and hands
- A mixing cup and stirring utensil
- Sandpaper

Start by cutting a wooden circle to the desired size for your clock. Place the wooden circle into the wooden mold, making sure it is level. Mix the resin according to the manufacturer's instructions, adding pigment if desired.

Pour the resin into the mold, making sure it covers the wooden circle completely. Use a torch or heat gun to remove any air bubbles that may have formed. Once cured, remove the clock from the mold and sand the surface of the resin until it is smooth and level with the wooden circle.

Install the clock mechanism and hands onto the wooden circle, following the manufacturer's instructions. Hang the clock on the wall and enjoy your beautiful resin and wood wall clock!

Woodworking with resin opens up a world of creative possibilities and allows for unique and stunning DIY projects. From a resin river coffee table to resin coasters, the projects listed above are engaging, practical, and beautiful. With a few materials and some creativity, you can create unique pieces of home decor or functional items that will be treasured for years to come. So, roll up your sleeves and get ready to create something beautiful!

Resin and wood wall clock

Resin Inlay Box

Create a beautiful wooden box and add intricate resin inlays to give it a unique and colorful touch.

To create a resin inlay box, you will need:

- Wooden box (pre-made or built from scratch)
- Resin
- Pigment (optional)
- Mixing cup and stirring utensil
- Small tools for creating resin patterns (e.g., toothpicks, small brushes)
- Sandpaper
- Finishing materials (e.g., varnish, wax)

Here are the steps to create a resin inlay box:

1. <u>Prepare the wooden box:</u> If you're using a pre-made wooden box, make sure it's clean and smooth. If you're building the box yourself, cut and assemble the wooden pieces to create the desired box shape.

2. <u>Plan your resin design:</u> Decide on the pattern or design you want to create with the resin inlays. You can draw it

directly on the box or create a template to guide your resin placement.

3. <u>Mix and tint the resin:</u> Follow the manufacturer's instructions to mix the resin. If desired, add pigments to achieve the desired colors for your resin inlays.

4. <u>Pour the resin:</u> Pour a small amount of resin into the designated areas of the box where you want the inlays to be. Use small tools like toothpicks or brushes to manipulate and spread the resin to create the desired patterns.

5. <u>Cure the resin:</u> Allow the resin to cure according to the manufacturer's instructions. This typically takes 24 to 48 hours. Make sure the box is placed in a well-ventilated area during the curing process.

6. <u>Sand and finish:</u> Once the resin is fully cured, use sandpaper to smooth any rough edges or uneven surfaces. 7. Apply a suitable finish, such as varnish or wax, to protect and enhance the beauty of the wooden box.

Inlay box

Resin Bookends

Design and create stylish bookends using a combination of wood and resin to add a decorative touch to your bookshelf.

To create resin bookends, you will need:

- Wood blocks (pre-made or cut from larger pieces)

- Resin
- Pigment (optional)
- Mixing cup and stirring utensil
- Small tools for resin manipulation (e.g., toothpicks, small brushes)
- Sandpaper
- Finishing materials (e.g., varnish, wax)

Steps to creating resin bookends:

1. <u>Prepare the wood blocks:</u> If you're using pre-made wood blocks, make sure they are clean and smooth. If you're cutting the blocks yourself, measure and cut the wood pieces to the desired size and shape for bookends.

2. <u>Design the resin inlays:</u> Decide on the resin patterns or designs you want to incorporate into the bookends. This could include swirling colors, geometric shapes, or other creative arrangements.

3. <u>Mix and tint the resin:</u> Mix the resin according to the manufacturer's instructions. Add pigments if desired to achieve the desired colors for your resin inlays.

4. <u>Pour the resin</u>: Pour a small amount of resin onto the wood blocks, where you want the inlays to be. Use small tools like toothpicks or brushes to manipulate the resin and create the desired patterns or designs.

5. <u>Cure the resin:</u> Allow the resin to cure fully according to the manufacturer's instructions. This typically takes 24 to 48 hours. Ensure the bookends are placed in a well-ventilated area during the curing process.

6. <u>Sand and finish:</u> Once the resin is fully cured, use sand finish, such as varnish or wax, to protect the wood and enhance its appearance.

Resin Picture Frames

You can make custom picture frames by embedding resin designs into wooden frames. This allows you to showcase your favorite photos in a truly personalized way.

To create resin picture frames, you will need:

- Wooden frames (pre-made or built from scratch)
- Resin
- Pigment (optional)
- Mixing cup and stirring utensil

- Small tools for resin manipulation (e.g., toothpicks, small brushes)
- Sandpaper
- Finishing materials (e.g., varnish, wax)

Here are the steps to create resin picture frames:

1. <u>Prepare the wooden frames:</u> If using pre-made frames, ensure they are clean and smooth. If building the frames yourself, cut and assemble the wooden pieces to create the desired frame shape and size.

2. <u>Design the resin inlays</u>: Determine the resin designs you want to incorporate into the frames. This could include abstract patterns, floral motifs, or any other creative ideas.

3. <u>Mix and tint the resin:</u> Mix the resin following the manufacturer's instructions. Optionally, add pigments to achieve the desired colors for your resin inlays.

4. <u>Pour the resin:</u> Pour a small amount of resin onto the wooden frames in the areas where you want the inlays to be. Use small tools like toothpicks or brushes to manipulate the resin and create the desired designs.

5. <u>Cure the resin:</u> Allow the resin to cure fully based on the manufacturer's instructions. This typically takes 24 to 48

hours. Place the frames in a well-ventilated area during the curing process.

6. Sand and finish: Once the resin is fully cured, use sandpaper to smooth any rough edges or uneven surfaces. Apply a suitable finish, such as varnish or wax, to protect and enhance the appearance of the wooden frames.

Picture frame

Resin Wall Shelf

Build a wooden wall shelf and incorporate resin accents to create a striking and functional display piece for your home.

To create a resin wall shelf, you will need:

- Wooden shelf boards (pre-made or cut from larger pieces)
- Resin
- Pigment (optional)
- Mixing cup and stirring utensil
- Small tools for resin manipulation (e.g., toothpicks, small brushes)
- Wall brackets and screws for mounting
- Sandpaper
- Finishing materials (e.g., varnish, wax)

Here are the steps to create a resin wall shelf:

1. Prepare the wooden shelf boards: If using pre-made shelf boards, ensure they are clean and smooth. If cutting

the boards yourself, measure and cut the wood to the desired size and shape for the shelf.

2. Design the resin accents: Decide on the resin accents you want to incorporate into the shelf. This could include flowing patterns, geometric shapes, or any other creative designs.

3. Mix and tint the resin: Mix the resin following the manufacturer's instructions. If desired, add pigments to achieve the desired colors for the resin accents.

4. Pour the resin: Pour the resin onto the designated areas of the wooden shelf boards, where you want the accents to be. Use small tools like toothpicks or brushes to manipulate the resin and create the desired designs.

5. Cure the resin: Allow the resin to cure fully based on the manufacturer's instructions. This typically takes 24 to 48 hours. Place the shelf boards in a well-ventilated area during the curing process.

6. Sand and finish: Once the resin is fully cured, use sandpaper to smooth any rough edges or uneven surfaces. Apply a suitable finish, such as varnish or wax, to protect the wood and resin and enhance the appearance of the wall shelf.

The Ultimate Guide to Woodworking with Resin

Wall shelf

CHAPTER 10

INNOVATIVE RESIN TECHNIQUES AND APPLICATIONS

Innovative resin techniques have revolutionized the world of crafting and art, offering endless possibilities for creativity and expression. Resin casting with molds, creating resin inlays, resin lamination and layering, resin sculpting and carving, and resin dyeing and coloring techniques are some of the exciting methods that allow artists and crafters to explore new horizons. In this chapter, we will look at each technique, providing step-by-step instructions and insights to help you master the art of resin crafting.

Resin Casting with Molds

Resin casting with molds is a popular technique that enables artists to create three-dimensional objects with stunning clarity and detail. Follow these steps to successfully cast resin using molds:

Step 1: Prepare your workspace

Ensure you have a clean and well-ventilated area to work in. Lay down a protective covering on your work surface to catch any spills or drips.

Step 2: Select a mold

Choose a mold that suits your desired shape and size. Silicone molds are commonly used for resin casting due to their flexibility and ease of use.

Step 3: Prepare the mold

Clean and dry the mold thoroughly to remove any dust or debris. If necessary, apply a mold release agent to facilitate easy removal of the cured resin.

Step 4: Mix the resin

Follow the manufacturer's instructions to mix the resin and catalyst in the correct ratio. Stir gently but thoroughly to avoid introducing air bubbles.

Step 5: Pour the resin

Carefully pour the mixed resin into the mold, ensuring it fills all the crevices and corners. Use a stir stick or toothpick to eliminate any air bubbles that may rise to the surface.

Step 6: Cure the resin

Allow the resin to cure according to the manufacturer's instructions. This typically involves leaving it undisturbed for a specific duration, usually 24 to 48 hours.

Step 7: Demold the casting

Once the resin is fully cured, gently flex the mold to release the casting. If the casting is stubborn, you can use a release agent or apply gentle pressure to facilitate its removal.

Creating Resin Inlays

Resin inlays are a fantastic way to add color, texture, and depth to your crafts. Follow these steps to create resin inlays that enhance your projects:

Step 1: Select a base material

Choose a suitable base material, such as wood, acrylic, or metal, where you want to embed the resin inlay.

Step 2: Prepare the base material

Clean and sand the surface of the base material to ensure it is smooth and free of imperfections. Wipe away any dust or debris.

Step 3: Create a recess

Using a chisel, Dremel tool, or router, create a recess or groove in the base material. Ensure the depth and shape of the recess accommodate the desired resin inlay.

Step 4: Mix the resin

Prepare the resin mixture according to the manufacturer's instructions. If desired, add pigments, glitters, or other additives to create unique effects.

Step 5: Pour the resin

Carefully pour the resin into the prepared recess, ensuring it fills the entire area. Use a toothpick or small brush to spread the resin evenly and eliminate any air bubbles.

Step 6: Cure the resin

Allow the resin to cure completely. Depending on the type of resin used, this may take anywhere from a few hours to a few days.

Step 7: Finish the surface

Once the resin is fully cured, sand the surface of the base material to remove any excess resin and achieve a smooth finish. Apply a protective coating if desired.

Creating resin inlay in woodwork

Resin Lamination and Layering

Resin lamination and layering techniques offer endless possibilities for creating captivating designs and patterns. Follow these steps to master resin lamination and layering:

Step 1: Prepare your workspace

Ensure you have a clean and level work surface. Lay down a protective covering to catch any spills or drips.

Step 2: Select your materials

Choose the materials you want to laminate or layer with resin. This can include paper, fabric, dried flowers, or any other thin and lightweight objects.

Step 3: Arrange the layers

Arrange the layers of materials in the desired pattern or design. Experiment with different combinations to create visually appealing effects.

Step 4: Prepare the resin

Mix the resin according to the manufacturer's instructions, ensuring an adequate quantity to cover all the layers.

Step 5: Apply the resin

Carefully pour the mixed resin over the layered materials, ensuring it covers them completely. Use a brush or spatula to spread the resin evenly and remove any air bubbles.

Step 6: Cure the resin

Allow the resin to cure according to the manufacturer's instructions. This typically involves leaving it undisturbed for a specific duration.

Step 7: Finishing touches

Once the resin is fully cured, trim any excess material if necessary. Sand the surface lightly to achieve a smooth finish and apply a protective coating if desired.

Resin Sculpting and Carving

Resin sculpting and carving techniques enable artists to create intricate and detailed resin artworks. Follow these steps to unleash your creativity through resin sculpting:

Step 1: Prepare your workspace

Ensure you have a clean and well-ventilated area to work in. Lay down a protective covering on your work surface to catch any spills or drips.

Step 2: Select a resin suitable for sculpting

Choose a resin specifically formulated for sculpting and carving. These resins typically have a longer working time and are more rigid when cured.

Step 3: Mix the resin

Follow the manufacturer's instructions to mix the resin and catalyst in the correct ratio. Stir gently but thoroughly to avoid introducing air bubbles.

Step 4: Sculpt the resin

Working quickly but carefully, shape the mixed resin using your hands, sculpting tools, or molds. Take advantage of the resin's malleability during the initial stages.

Step 5: Refine the sculpture

Once the resin begins to cure and firm up, use carving tools to refine the details and create the desired textures. Take breaks if necessary to allow the resin to cure further.

Step 6: Cure the sculpture

Allow the resin sculpture to cure completely according to the manufacturer's instructions. This may involve leaving it undisturbed for a specific duration.

Step 7: Finishing touches

Once the sculpture is fully cured, sand the surface lightly to smooth out any imperfections. Apply a protective coating or polish the surface for a glossy finish.

Resin Dyeing and Coloring Techniques

Resin dyeing and coloring techniques allow artists to add vibrant hues and unique effects to their resin creations. Follow these steps to master resin dyeing and coloring:

Select your coloring agents

Choose from a variety of coloring agents such as liquid dyes, powdered pigments, alcohol inks, or even acrylic paints. Ensure the chosen coloring agents are compatible with resin.

Prepare the resin

Mix the resin and catalyst according to the manufacturer's instructions. If necessary, divide the resin into separate containers for different colors or effects.

Add the coloring agent

Slowly add a small amount of the coloring agent to the resin and stir gently. Add more color as needed to achieve the desired hue or effect. Remember, a little goes a long way.

Mix thoroughly

Stir the resin and coloring agent mixture thoroughly to ensure an even distribution of color. Take care not to introduce air bubbles during the mixing process.

Pour or apply the colored resin

Carefully pour the colored resin into molds, onto surfaces, or use it for various resin techniques as desired. Spread the resin evenly using a brush or spatula.

Cure the resin

Allow the colored resin to cure according to the manufacturer's instructions. The curing time will depend on the type of resin used.

Evaluate and refine

Once the resin is fully cured, evaluate the colors and effects achieved. If desired, you can apply additional layers of colored resin or further refine the piece with additional techniques.

By following the step-by-step instructions outlined in this chapter, you can unlock your creativity and explore innovative resin techniques and applications. Ensure you experiment, practice, and let your imagination soar as you work on your projects.

Lamination and Layering

The Ultimate Guide to Woodworking with Resin

Demonstrating the process of creating resin inlays in wood

CHAPTER 11

EXPLORING SPECIALIZED RESIN PRODUCTS FOR WOODWORKING

Woodworking is a timeless craft that has evolved over centuries, and the introduction of specialized resin products has opened up new possibilities for enhancing and protecting wooden creations.here, we will explore the use of specialized resin products specifically designed for woodworking, highlighting epoxy resin, polyester resin, UV resin, resin adhesives, and bonding agents, as well as resin fillers and reinforcements. Each of these products offers unique features and benefits that can take your woodworking projects to new heights of beauty and durability.

Epoxy Resin for Woodworking

Epoxy resin is a versatile and popular choice among woodworkers due to its exceptional strength, clarity, and resistance to moisture and heat. Here are the unique features and steps involved in using epoxy resin for woodworking:

Unique Features of Epoxy Resin

<u>Strong adhesion:</u> Epoxy resin forms a strong bond with wood, making it ideal for laminating, filling gaps, and stabilizing wooden surfaces.

<u>High clarity and UV resistance:</u> Epoxy resin is known for its ability to maintain a crystal-clear finish even when exposed to sunlight. It resists yellowing and protects the wood from UV damage.

<u>Self-leveling properties:</u> Epoxy resin has self-leveling characteristics, ensuring a smooth and even surface when applied correctly.

Steps for Using Epoxy Resin in Woodworking

Step 1: Surface preparation: Ensure that the wood surface is clean, dry, and free from any dust, grease, or contaminants. Sand the surface to create a rough texture for better adhesion.

Step 2: Mixing the epoxy resin: Follow the manufacturer's instructions to mix the epoxy resin and its hardener in the correct ratio. Use a clean container and mix thoroughly but gently to avoid introducing air bubbles.

Step 3: Applying the epoxy resin: Pour the mixed epoxy resin onto the wood surface. Use a brush or a spreader to evenly distribute the resin and ensure it covers the entire area. Tilt the surface if necessary to achieve a uniform coating.

Step 4: Removing air bubbles: Use a heat gun or a propane torch held at a safe distance to remove any air bubbles that may have formed during the application. Pass the heat source quickly over the surface to prevent overheating.

Step 5: Curing process: Allow the epoxy resin to cure according to the manufacturer's instructions. This typically involves leaving it undisturbed for a specific duration. Ensure the curing environment is clean and dust-free.

Step 6: Sanding and finishing: Once the epoxy resin is fully cured, sand the surface to achieve the desired smoothness. Apply a suitable finish, such as varnish or polyurethane, to protect and enhance the wood.

A resin river table

Polyester Resin for Woodworking

Polyester resin is another popular choice for woodworking projects, offering different characteristics and benefits compared to epoxy resin. Let's explore the unique features and steps involved in using polyester resin for woodworking:

Unique Features of Polyester Resin:

Fast curing time: Polyester resin cures relatively quickly, allowing for faster project completion and reduced waiting time.

Cost-effective: Polyester resin is generally more affordable compared to epoxy resin, making it a budget-friendly option for woodworking projects.

Excellent filling properties: Polyester resin has good gap-filling capabilities, making it suitable for repairing cracks, knots, or voids in wood.

Steps for Using Polyester Resin in Woodworking

Step 1: Surface preparation: Prepare the wood surface by cleaning it thoroughly and ensuring it is dry and free from dust or contaminants.

Step 2: Mixing the polyester resin: Follow the manufacturer's instructions to mix the polyester resin with its catalyst in the correct ratio. Use a clean container and stir the mixture thoroughly but gently.

Step 3: Applying the polyester resin: Pour the mixed polyester resin onto the wood surface or into the desired areas that require filling or reinforcement. Use a brush or spatula to spread the resin and ensure it fills the gaps or covers the necessary areas.

Step 4: Curing process: Polyester resin typically cures within a few hours, but the exact curing time may vary depending on factors such as temperature and humidity. Allow the resin to cure completely before proceeding with further steps.

Step 5: Sanding and finishing: Once the polyester resin is fully cured, sand the surface to achieve a smooth and even finish. Apply a suitable finish, such as varnish or lacquer, to protect and enhance the wood.

UV Resin for Woodworking

UV resin is a relatively new and innovative product in the woodworking world, offering unique advantages for certain applications. Let's explore the features and steps involved in using UV resin for woodworking:

UV Resin Features

<u>Instant curing with UV light:</u> UV resin cures almost instantly when exposed to UV light, allowing for rapid project completion and reduced waiting time.

Precise control: UV resin remains liquid until exposed to UV light, giving woodworkers precise control over the curing process and allowing for intricate designs and effects.

Low odor and low VOCs: UV resin typically has low odor and low levels of volatile organic compounds, making it a favorable option for those concerned about the environmental impact.

Steps for Using UV Resin in Woodworking

Step 1: Surface preparation: Prepare the wood surface by cleaning it thoroughly and ensuring it is dry and free from dust or contaminants.

Step 2: Applying the UV resin: Using a brush, dropper, or other suitable application method, apply the UV resin to the desired areas of the wood. Take care to avoid excess resin or drips.

Step 3: Spreading and shaping: Use a brush or spatula to spread and shape the UV resin as desired. Take advantage of the resin's liquid state to create unique designs or fill intricate details.

Step 4: Curing process: Once you are satisfied with the resin application, expose the wood to UV light using a UV lamp or natural sunlight. Follow the manufacturer's instructions for the appropriate exposure time.

Step 5: Final touches: Once the UV resin is fully cured, check for any imperfections or rough edges. Sand the surface lightly if necessary, and apply a suitable finish to protect the wood and enhance the resin's appearance.

Resin Adhesives and Bonding Agents

Resin adhesives and bonding agents play a crucial role in woodworking projects, ensuring strong and durable bonds between wood pieces. Let's explore the features and steps involved in using resin adhesives and bonding agents:

Unique Features of Resin Adhesives and Bonding Agents

Strong and durable bonds: Resin adhesives create strong and long-lasting bonds between wood pieces, enhancing the structural integrity of the project.

Gap-filling capabilities: Resin adhesives with gap-filling properties help compensate for irregularities or gaps in the wood surfaces, ensuring a solid connection.

<u>Water and heat resistance:</u> Many resin adhesives are resistant to water and heat, making them suitable for outdoor or high-temperature applications.

Steps for Using Resin Adhesives and Bonding Agents:

Step 1: Surface preparation: Prepare the wood surfaces to be bonded by ensuring they are clean, dry, and free from any contaminants or finishes.

Step 2: Apply the resin adhesive: Using a brush, roller, or suitable application method, apply the resin adhesive to one or both surfaces to be bonded. Follow the manufacturer's instructions for the recommended coverage.

Step 3: Joining the wood pieces: Press the wood pieces together firmly, ensuring even pressure across the entire joint. Wipe off any excess adhesive that may squeeze out from the joint.

Step 4: Curing time: Allow the resin adhesive to cure according to the manufacturer's instructions. This may involve clamping the wood pieces together to maintain pressure during the curing process.

Step 5: Final finishing: Once the resin adhesive is fully cured, sand the surface if necessary to achieve a smooth finish. Apply a suitable finish or sealant to protect the wood and enhance the bond.

A polyester resin piece

Resin Fillers and Reinforcements

Resin fillers and reinforcements are essential for strengthening, repairing, and enhancing the characteristics of wood. Let's explore the features and steps involved in using resin fillers and reinforcements:

Unique Features of Resin Fillers and Reinforcements

Strength and durability: Resin fillers and reinforcements significantly increase the strength and durability of wood, making it suitable for high-stress applications or repairs.

Gap-filling properties: Resin fillers are often used to fill voids, cracks, or knots in wood, providing a solid and stable surface for further woodworking processes.

Compatibility with different resins: Resin fillers and reinforcements are designed to be compatible with various resin systems, allowing for seamless integration into woodworking projects.

Steps for Using Resin Fillers and Reinforcements

Step 1: Surface preparation: Prepare the wood surface by cleaning it thoroughly and ensuring it is dry and free from dust or contaminants.

Step 2: Mixing the resin filler or reinforcement: Follow the manufacturer's instructions to mix the resin filler or reinforcement with the corresponding resin system in the recommended ratio.

Step 3: Applying the resin filler or reinforcement: Use a brush, spatula, or suitable application method to apply the resin filler or reinforcement to the desired areas. Ensure it fills the gaps or covers the necessary surfaces.

Step 4: Curing process: Allow the resin filler or reinforcement to cure according to the manufacturer's instructions. This may involve leaving it undisturbed for a specific duration or applying heat if necessary.

Step 5: Sanding and finishing: Once the resin filler or reinforcement is fully cured, sand the surface to achieve a smooth and even finish. Apply a suitable finish or sealant to protect the wood and enhance the resin's appearance.

In sum, specialized resin products for woodworking, such as epoxy resin, polyester resin, UV resin, resin adhesives, and bonding agents, as well as resin fillers and reinforcements, offer woodworkers a wide range of options to enhance, protect, and create stunning wooden creations. Understanding the unique features and steps involved in using these resin products allows woodworkers to explore new techniques, improve the strength and durability of their projects, and unleash their creativity. Experimentation and practice will help you master the art of using specialized resin products for woodworking, taking your craftsmanship to the next level.

Another sample polyester resin woodwork

A sleek resin woodwork piece

CHAPTER 12

ADVANCED FINISHING TECHNIQUES AND SURFACE TREATMENTS

Finishing techniques and surface treatments are critical aspects of any woodworking project, as they not only enhance the appearance but also protect the wood and create a durable and long-lasting finish. In this chapter, we will focus on advanced finishing techniques and surface treatments that can take your woodworking projects to a new level of beauty and sophistication. Some of the things we will discuss include: high-gloss polishing and buffing, matte and satin finishes, resin sanding and smoothing techniques, resin staining and aging effects, as well as resin surface coatings and protective layers. These techniques will help you achieve professional-grade results and showcase your woodworking skills.

High-Gloss Polishing and Buffing

High-gloss finishes offer a stunning, mirror-like appearance that enhances the beauty of the wood and creates a luxurious look. Polishing and buffing techniques play a crucial role in achieving a high-gloss finish. The following are the steps involved in high-gloss polishing and buffing:

Step 1: Surface preparation: Ensure that the wood surface is clean, dry, and free from any dust, grease, or contaminants. Sand the surface gradually with increasingly finer grit sandpaper to achieve a smooth finish.

Step 2: Application of finishing products: Apply a suitable clear coat or finish to the wood surface, such as polyurethane, lacquer, or varnish. Follow the manufacturer's instructions for the recommended application method and drying time.

Step 3: Sanding between coats: After each coat of finish has dried, lightly sand the surface with fine-grit sandpaper to remove any imperfections or raised grain. Wipe off the dust with a clean cloth or tack cloth.

Step 4: Buffing process: Use a buffing wheel or a polishing pad attached to a drill or buffer machine. Apply a high-quality polishing compound to the buffing wheel and gently move it across the wood surface in a circular motion. Continue buffing until a glossy shine is achieved.

Step 5: Final touch: After buffing, wipe the wood surface with a clean, soft cloth to remove any residue or excess polishing compound. Inspect the finish for any imperfections and touch up if necessary.

A wooden surface with a high gloss finish

Matte and Satin Finishes

Matte and satin finishes offer an elegant and subtle look that can enhance the natural beauty of the wood while providing a smooth, non-reflective surface. Let's explore the steps involved in achieving matte and satin finishes:

Step 1: Surface preparation: Prepare the wood surface by cleaning it thoroughly and ensuring it is dry and free from dust or contaminants.

Step 2: Application of finishing products: Apply a suitable matte or satin finish to the wood surface, such as a matte varnish, matte lacquer, or satin polyurethane. Follow the manufacturer's instructions for the recommended application method and drying time.

Step 3: Sanding between coats: After each coat of finish has dried, lightly sand the surface with fine-grit sandpaper to remove any imperfections or raised grain. Wipe off the dust with a clean cloth or tack cloth.

Step 4: Repeat the application: Apply multiple coats of the matte or satin finish, allowing each coat to dry completely before applying the next. The number of coats will depend on the desired level of sheen and protection.

Step 5: Final touch: Once the final coat has dried, inspect the surface for any imperfections or rough areas. Lightly sand the surface if necessary and apply a suitable wax or polish to enhance the finish and provide additional protection.

Resin sanding and smoothing

Resin Sanding and Smoothing Techniques

Resin sanding and smoothing techniques are essential for achieving a smooth and flawless surface on resin-coated wood. Let's explore the steps involved in resin sanding and smoothing techniques:

Step 1: Surface preparation: Prepare the resin-coated wood surface by cleaning it thoroughly and ensuring it is dry. If there are any rough areas or imperfections, use a scraper or sandpaper to level the surface.

Step 2: Coarse sanding: Start with coarse-grit sandpaper (around 120 to 150 grit) to remove any major imperfections or unevenness. Sand in a circular or back-and-forth motion, applying even pressure across the surface.

Step 3: Progress to finer grits: Gradually progress to finer-grit sandpaper (such as 220, 320, and 400 grit) to achieve a smoother surface. Continue sanding in the same motion, ensuring even pressure and consistent sanding.

Step 4: Wet sanding: For an even smoother finish, wet sand the surface using fine-grit sandpaper (around 600 to

1200 grit). Keep the surface and sandpaper wet with water or a sanding lubricant to reduce friction and prevent clogging.

Step 5: Polishing and buffing: After the surface is thoroughly dry, use a polishing compound or resin-specific polishing products to further enhance the shine and smoothness. Apply the compound to a soft cloth and gently buff the resin surface.

Resin Staining and Aging Effects

Resin staining and aging effects can add depth, character, and a weathered appearance to your woodworking projects. Let's explore the steps involved in resin staining and aging effects:

Step 1: Surface preparation: Prepare the wood surface by cleaning it thoroughly and ensuring it is dry. If desired, you can lightly sand the surface to create a slightly rough texture for better adhesion.

Step 2: Choose a stain or coloring agent: Select a suitable stain or coloring agent that is compatible with resin. You can choose from a variety of options such as liquid dyes, pigments, or specialized resin stains.

Step 3: Apply the stain: Using a brush, sponge, or cloth, apply the stain or coloring agent to the wood surface, focusing on areas where you want the aging effects to be more pronounced. Allow the stain to penetrate the wood and dry according to the manufacturer's instructions.

Step 4: Apply resin: Once the stain has dried, apply a layer of resin over the stained wood surface. Use a brush or spreader to evenly distribute the resin and ensure it covers the entire area.

Step 5: Create aging effects: While the resin is still wet, you can manipulate the surface to create desired aging effects. You can use a heat gun, blowtorch, or other tools to create cracks, bubbles, or textures in the resin. Experiment with different techniques to achieve the desired effect.

Step 6: Curing process: Allow the resin to cure according to the manufacturer's instructions. This typically involves leaving it undisturbed for a specific duration. Ensure the curing environment is clean and dust-free.

Resin staining and aging effects

Resin Surface Coatings and Protective Layers

Resin surface coatings and protective layers are crucial for preserving the beauty and durability of woodworking projects. Let's explore the steps involved in applying resin surface coatings and protective layers:

Step 1: Surface preparation: Prepare the wood surface by cleaning it thoroughly and ensuring it is dry. If necessary, lightly sand the surface to create a slightly rough texture for better adhesion.

Step 2: Choose a suitable resin coating: Select a resin coating that is specifically designed for woodworking projects. Consider factors such as clarity, UV resistance, and the desired level of protection.

Step 3: Mixing and applying resin: Follow the manufacturer's instructions to mix the resin and its hardener in the correct ratio. Use a clean container and mix thoroughly but gently to avoid introducing air bubbles. Apply the resin to the wood surface using a brush, roller, or other suitable application method.

Step 4: Spreading and leveling: Use a brush or spreader to evenly spread the resin over the wood surface, ensuring complete coverage. Pay attention to any edges or corners to avoid uneven coating. Use a torch or heat gun to remove any air bubbles that may have formed.

Step 5: Curing process: Allow the resin to cure according to the manufacturer's instructions. This may involve leaving it undisturbed for a specific duration. Ensure the curing environment is clean and dust-free.

Step 6: Sanding and additional layers: Once the initial layer of resin has cured, sand the surface lightly to remove any imperfections or rough areas. Apply additional layers of resin as needed to achieve the desired thickness and level of protection.

Advanced finishing techniques and surface treatments play a crucial role in elevating the beauty and durability of woodworking projects. High-gloss polishing and buffing, matte and satin finishes, resin sanding and smoothing techniques, resin staining and aging effects, as well as resin surface coatings and protective layers, provide woodworkers with a wide range of options to achieve professional-grade results. By mastering these techniques and using suitable products, you can transform ordinary wood into stunning, visually appealing creations that will stand the test of time.

Working with resin brings out creativity

CHAPTER 13

MAINTENANCE AND CARE

Woodworking with resin is an increasingly popular technique among DIY enthusiasts and professional woodworkers alike. The combination of wood and resin can create stunning and unique pieces that are both durable and aesthetically pleasing. However, to ensure that your woodworking with resin projects stand the test of time, it's important to know how to properly maintain and care for them. I will sharing some tips to help you keep your woodworking with resin projects in tip-top shape.

Understanding the Characteristics of Resin

Before diving into maintenance and care tips, it's important to have a basic understanding of resin and its properties. Resin is a synthetic polymer that, when combined with a hardener, creates a hard and durable material. There are many types of resin available on the market, but the most commonly used in woodworking is epoxy resin. Epoxy resin is a two-part system that consists of a resin and a hardener. When mixed together, the two parts chemically react to form a hard and durable material.

One of the key characteristics of epoxy resin is its high resistance to water and chemicals. This makes it an ideal material for use in woodworking projects, particularly those that will be exposed to moisture or chemicals. Epoxy resin also has excellent adhesion properties, meaning it can bond strongly with a variety of surfaces, including wood.

However, epoxy resin is not without its drawbacks. One of the main issues with epoxy resin is that it can yellow over time when exposed to UV light. This can detract from the overall appearance of your woodworking with resin projects. Additionally, epoxy resin can be brittle and prone to cracking if not properly cured.

With these characteristics in mind, let's take a look at some tips for maintaining and caring for your woodworking with resin projects.

Tips for Maintaining and Caring for Woodworking with Resin

1. Keep your woodworking with resin projects out of direct sunlight

As we mentioned earlier, epoxy resin can yellow over time when exposed to UV light. To prevent this from happening, it's important to keep your woodworking with resin projects out of direct sunlight as much as possible. If your project must be exposed to sunlight, consider using a UV-resistant coating to protect it.

2. Use a non-abrasive cleaner

When cleaning your woodworking with resin projects, it's important to use a non-abrasive cleaner to avoid scratching the surface. Avoid using harsh chemicals or abrasive materials, as these can damage the resin and the wood. Instead, use a mild soap and water solution or a specialized cleaner designed for use on epoxy resin.

3. Avoid exposing your woodworking with resin projects to extreme temperatures

Epoxy resin can be sensitive to extreme temperatures, so it's important to avoid exposing your woodworking with resin projects to temperatures outside of the recommended range. Check the manufacturer's instructions for the recommended temperature range for your particular resin and avoid exposing your project to temperatures outside of this range.

4. Store your woodworking with resin projects properly

If you need to store your woodworking with resin projects for an extended period of time, it's important to store them properly to prevent damage. Keep them in a dry, cool place and avoid stacking heavy objects on top of them. If possible, cover them with a protective layer to prevent dust and dirt from accumulating.

5. Repair any damage promptly

If your woodworking with resin project becomes damaged, it's important to repair it promptly to prevent the damage from spreading. Depending on the severity of the damage, you may be able to repair it yourself using a specialized resin repair kit or you may need to seek professional assistance.

6. Apply a protective coating

To help protect your woodworking with resin projects from scratches and other damage, consider applying a protective coating. There are many types of protective coatings available on the market, including polyurethane, lacquer, and wax. Before applying any coating, make sure to thoroughly clean and dry the surface to ensure good adhesion. Apply the coating according to the manufacturer's instructions and allow it to fully cure before using or storing your project.

7. Handle your woodworking with resin projects with care

When handling your woodworking with resin projects, it's important to handle them with care to prevent damage. Avoid dropping or bumping them, as this can cause cracks or other damage to the resin and wood. When moving or transporting your project, consider using protective padding or covers to prevent damage.

8. Regularly inspect your woodworking with resin projects

To ensure that your woodworking with resin projects remain in good condition, it's important to regularly inspect them for any signs of damage or wear. Check for cracks, scratches, or other damage and address any issues promptly to prevent further damage.

Working on wood projects with resin can be a rewarding and creative endeavor, but it's important to properly maintain and care for your projects to ensure they last for years to come. By following these tips and techniques, you can help protect your woodwork from damage and keep them looking their best. Remember to handle your projects with care, keep them out of direct sunlight, and regularly inspect them for signs of wear and tear.

Pouring resin in a cup

CHAPTER 14

HEALTH AND SAFETY CONSIDERATIONS IN WOODWORKING WITH RESIN

Woodworking with resin is a fascinating and creative activity that allows woodworkers to create unique and beautiful pieces of art. However, like any woodworking project, working with resin comes with its own set of health and safety considerations that must be taken into account to protect both the woodworker and those around them. Now, let's discuss the important health and safety considerations that woodworkers must keep in mind when working with resin.

Respiratory Protection

One of the most important health and safety considerations when working with resin is respiratory protection. Most resins emit volatile organic compounds (VOCs) during the curing process, which can be harmful if inhaled. These VOCs can cause a range of health issues, including headaches, dizziness, nausea, and respiratory problems. Therefore, it is important to wear proper respiratory protection, such as a respirator or a mask with a filter, when working with resin.

When choosing a respirator, it is important to select one that is rated for use with VOCs. Look for a respirator with a rating of at least N95 or P100, which indicates that it can filter out 95% or more of airborne particles. A full-face respirator is also a good choice, as it provides eye and face protection as well as respiratory protection.

If you are working in a poorly ventilated area or using large amounts of resin, it may also be necessary to use an air purifying respirator or a supplied air respirator. An air purifying respirator uses filters to remove contaminants from the air, while a supplied air respirator provides clean air from a remote source.

Eye and Face Protection

In addition to respiratory protection, eye and face protection are also important when working with resin.

Resin can cause eye and skin irritation if it comes into contact with these areas. Therefore, it is important to wear safety glasses or goggles to protect your eyes from resin splashes or spills.

If you are working with a large amount of resin or using a spray gun, it may be necessary to wear a full-face shield to protect your face from resin particles. In addition, it is important to wear gloves to protect your hands from resin exposure.

Skin Protection

Resin can also cause skin irritation and allergic reactions. Therefore, it is important to protect your skin from contact with resin. Wear long-sleeved shirts and pants to cover your skin, and avoid wearing clothing that can absorb resin, such as cotton.

If you do get resin on your skin, wash the affected area with soap and water immediately. If you experience any skin irritation or allergic reactions, seek medical attention.

Ventilation

Proper ventilation is another important health and safety consideration when working with resin. Resins emit VOCs that can be harmful if inhaled in high concentrations. Therefore, it is important to work in a well-ventilated area or use a ventilation system to remove fumes and maintain safe air quality.

If you are working indoors, make sure to open windows and doors to allow for proper air flow. A fan or air purifier can also help to circulate air and remove fumes. If you are working in a confined space or using large amounts of resin, it may be necessary to use a ventilation system, such as a fume hood or exhaust fan, to remove fumes and maintain safe air quality.

Fire Safety

Resin is flammable and can ignite if exposed to high heat or open flames. Therefore, it is important to take proper fire safety precautions when working with resin. Do not smoke or use open flames near resin, and make sure to store resin away from heat sources.

In addition, it is important to have a fire extinguisher on hand in case of a fire. Make sure the fire extinguisher is rated for use with flammable liquids and that you know how to use it properly.

Another important fire safety consideration is the use of electrical equipment. When using power tools or other electrical equipment near resin, make sure the equipment is in good condition and that the cords are not frayed or damaged. Do not use equipment with exposed wires or damaged plugs, as this can increase the risk of electrical shock or fire.

Proper Storage and Handling

Proper storage and handling of resin is also important for health and safety. Store resin in a cool, dry place away from direct sunlight and heat sources. Make sure to keep resin containers tightly closed when not in use to prevent spills or leaks.

When handling resin, make sure to follow the manufacturer's instructions carefully. Use only the recommended amount of hardener, and mix resin and hardener thoroughly before use. Do not mix more resin than you can use within the recommended pot life, as this can cause the resin to overheat and cure too quickly.

Dispose of resin and hardener properly, following local regulations and guidelines. Do not pour resin down the drain or dispose of it in the trash, as this can harm the environment.

Training and Education

Proper training and education are essential for ensuring health and safety when working with resin. Woodworkers should be trained in the proper use of respirators, eye and face protection, and other safety equipment. They should also be educated on the potential hazards of resin and how to prevent exposure.

It is also important to stay up-to-date on the latest safety guidelines and regulations related to working with resin. Attend workshops, seminars, and other training events to learn about new safety measures and best practices.

Working with resin can be a rewarding and creative activity for woodworkers, but it also comes with important health and safety considerations. Proper respiratory protection, eye and face protection, skin protection, ventilation, fire safety, and storage and handling are all essential for protecting woodworkers and those around them from the potential hazards of resin.

By following these guidelines and staying up-to-date on the latest safety measures and regulations, woodworkers can enjoy the benefits of working with resin while ensuring the health and safety of themselves and others.

Remember to always prioritize safety when working with resin, and do not hesitate to seek medical attention if you experience any adverse health effects.

Safety first

The Ultimate Guide to Woodworking with Resin

CHAPTER 15

INSPIRATION AND RESOURCES FOR WOODWORKING WITH RESIN

Woodworking with resin is a popular and exciting trend in the woodworking community. Combining the natural beauty of wood with the glossy and colorful texture of resin creates stunning pieces that are both functional and aesthetic. No matter your level of experience in working with wood, there are plenty of ways to get inspired and find resources for woodworking with resin.

Inspiration

One of the best ways to get inspired for woodworking with resin is to browse social media platforms such as Instagram and Pinterest. On these platforms, you'll find a wealth of photos and videos showcasing the latest techniques and designs for woodworking with resin. By following accounts that specialize in woodworking with resin, you'll be exposed to an endless stream of ideas and inspiration.

Another great way to get inspired is to attend woodworking events such as trade shows or workshops. These events offer an opportunity to connect with other woodworkers and learn from the experts. You'll be able to see firsthand the latest tools and techniques for woodworking with resin and get inspired by the work of other talented artisans.

If you're looking for inspiration beyond social media and events, consider exploring different types of wood and resin combinations. For example, try experimenting with different color pigments or additives to create unique textures and patterns. Additionally, consider incorporating other materials such as metal or glass into your resin-wood projects for added dimension and interest.

Resources

Once you're inspired and ready to dive into woodworking with resin, it's important to have the right resources at your disposal. Here are a few practical resources to help you get started:

a. Woodworking with Resin Books and Magazines

There are a variety of books and magazines that specialize in woodworking with resin. These resources offer step-by-step instructions for different projects, as well as tips and techniques for working with different types of resin and wood. Some popular options include "Woodworking with Resin" by Peter Brown and "Resin Art: Beyond the Basics" by Kristen Unger.

b. Online Tutorials

There are countless online tutorials available for woodworking with resin. Websites such as YouTube offer a wide range of videos that cover everything from basic techniques to advanced projects. By watching these tutorials, you'll gain valuable insights into the best practices for working with resin, as well as creative ideas for different projects.

c. Resin and Woodworking Supplies

When it comes to woodworking with resin, it's important to have the right supplies. This includes everything from the resin itself to the tools needed for shaping and finishing your projects. There are a variety of online suppliers that specialize in woodworking with resin, such as Resin Obsession, ArtResin, and Just Resin. These suppliers offer a wide range of products, including resin, pigments, molds, and tools.

d. Woodworking with Resin Communities

Joining a community of like-minded woodworkers can be a great way to learn from others and share your own experiences. There are a variety of online communities dedicated to woodworking with resin, such as Facebook groups and forums. By joining these communities, you'll be able to ask questions, share your own projects, and connect with other woodworkers who share your passion.

More Valuable Tips and Techniques

Woodworking with resin can be a challenging process, but with the right guidance, you can ensure that your projects turn out beautifully. Here are a few practical tips to keep in mind:

Choose the Right Wood

When selecting wood for your resin projects, it's important to choose a type of wood that will work well with resin. Some woods are more porous than others, which can make it more difficult for the resin to adhere properly. Hardwoods such as maple, walnut, and oak are good options for resin projects, as they are less porous and provide a smooth surface for the resin.

Prepare Your Workspace

Before starting your resin project, it's important to prepare your workspace properly. This includes ensuring that you have adequate ventilation, as resin can emit fumes that can be harmful if inhaled. Additionally, make sure to protect your workspace by covering it with plastic or wax paper, as resin can be difficult to clean up if spilled.

Measure and Mix Carefully

When working with resin, it's important to measure and mix the components carefully. Resin typically consists of two parts – a resin and a hardener – that need to be mixed in specific ratios. Make sure to follow the instructions carefully and measure out the components accurately to ensure that the resin sets properly.

Experiment with Pigments and Additives

One of the fun aspects of woodworking with resin is the ability to experiment with different pigments and additives to create unique effects. Consider adding mica powder or glitter to create a sparkling effect, or using alcohol inks to create colorful patterns. Additionally, you can experiment with different types of wood stains or dyes to create interesting color combinations.

Sand and Polish Your Project

After the resin has set, it's important to sand and polish your project to achieve a smooth, glossy finish. Start with a coarse grit sandpaper and work your way up to a finer grit, ensuring that you sand evenly and carefully to avoid damaging the resin. Once the sanding is complete, use a polishing compound and a buffing wheel to achieve a high shine.

Woodworking with resin offers a creative way to combine natural wood with the vibrant and glossy texture of resin. By exploring different sources of inspiration and utilizing practical resources such as books, online tutorials, and community forums, you can gain the skills and knowledge needed to create beautiful and unique resin-wood projects.

Printable PDF File

As a way of ensuring you get maximum value from this book, I have added a printable PDF version, containing colored pictures. You can view, download or print the file. Just scan the QR code below to get access to it, at no extra cost.

Beauty and creativity of woodworking with resin

GLOSSARY

Abrasion - The process of wearing down or smoothing a surface using a tool or abrasive material.

Adhesive - A substance used to bond two materials together.

Catalyst - A substance that initiates or accelerates a chemical reaction.

Cavity - A hole or depression in a surface.

Clamping - The process of securing two pieces of material together using a clamp or other tool.

Clear resin - A transparent or translucent liquid used in resin casting that cures to a hard, durable finish.

Coating - A layer of material applied to a surface for protection or decoration.

Colorant - A substance used to add color to a material.

Comb - A tool used to spread and comb through resin or other materials.

Composite - A material made from two or more different materials that are combined to create a new material with different properties.

Curing - The process of hardening and setting a material using heat, light, or a chemical reaction.

Dam - A barrier used to contain or control the flow of resin or other materials.

De-molding - The process of removing a cured resin piece from a mold or form.

Degassing - The process of removing air bubbles from resin or other materials using a vacuum chamber.

Depth gauge - A tool used to measure the depth of a hole or cavity.

Epoxy - A type of adhesive resin that is highly durable and resistant to water and chemicals.

Filler - A substance used to fill in gaps or cracks in a surface.

Finish - A coating applied to a surface for protection or decoration.

Flow - The movement or spreading of resin or other materials.

Gel time - The amount of time it takes for a resin to thicken and become gel-like before curing.

Hardener - A substance used to initiate or accelerate the curing process of a resin.

Inlay - A decorative technique where a material is set into a surface.

Joint - A connection between two pieces of material.

Lamination - The process of bonding two or more layers of material together to create a new material with different properties.

Mold - A form used to shape and contain resin or other materials.

Mixing ratio - The ratio of resin to hardener used in a particular resin system.

Opaque resin - A colored or pigmented resin that is not transparent or translucent.

Pigment - A substance used to add color to a material.

Pouring - The process of filling a mold or form with resin or other materials.

Pot life - The amount of time a resin remains usable after being mixed.

Pressure pot - A container used to apply pressure to resin or other materials during the curing process.

Release agent - A substance used to prevent resin or other materials from sticking to a mold or form.

Resin - A liquid polymer that can be cast, molded, or laminated to create a solid object.

Sanding - The process of smoothing and shaping a surface using sandpaper or other abrasive materials.

Sealant - A substance used to seal gaps or cracks in a surface.

Shaping - The process of forming a material into a desired shape.

Solvent - A substance used to dissolve or thin out resin or other materials.

Stabilization - The process of impregnating wood with resin or other materials to make it stronger, more durable, and resistant to decay.

Surface tension - The property of a liquid that causes it to minimize its surface area

Tack-free time - The amount of time it takes for a resin to become dry and no longer sticky to the touch.

Tint - A small amount of pigment used to color resin or other materials.

UV stabilizer - A substance used to protect resin or other materials from UV damage.

Viscosity - The thickness or resistance to flow of a liquid.

Void - An empty space or gap in a material.

Wet sanding - The process of sanding a surface while it is still wet with water or other liquid.

Wood stabilizing - The process of treating wood with resin or other materials to prevent warping, cracking, or decay.

Abrasive paper - A type of sandpaper with a rough surface for sanding and smoothing surfaces.

Acetone - A common solvent used to clean up resin or other materials.

Backfill - The process of filling in gaps or cracks in a surface with a resin or other material.

Casting - The process of pouring resin into a mold to create a solid object.

Chisel - A sharp tool used for cutting and shaping wood.

Crazing - The appearance of small cracks or lines on the surface of a material.

Density - The measure of mass per unit volume of a material.

Epoxy putty - A type of two-part epoxy resin that can be shaped and molded like putty.

Fiberglass - A composite material made from glass fibers and resin.

Grain - The direction and pattern of wood fibers on the surface of a piece of wood.

Hardness - The measure of a material's resistance to indentation or scratching.

Heat gun - A tool used to apply heat to a surface for shaping or drying.

Infiltration - The process of filling voids or spaces within a material with a resin or other material.

Joinery - The process of joining two or more pieces of wood together.

Kiln - A furnace used for drying and curing materials.

Laminate - A thin layer of material bonded to the surface of another material.

Mesh - A type of material made from woven fibers used for filtering or reinforcement.

Moisture content - The amount of water or moisture present in a material.

Non-toxic - A material that does not contain harmful or poisonous substances.

Overcoat - A protective layer applied on top of a finish.

Penetrating epoxy - A type of epoxy resin that penetrates deep into wood fibers to strengthen and stabilize them.

Polymerization - The process of linking monomer molecules together to form a polymer.

Reinforcement - A material added to a composite material to increase its strength and durability.

Router - A power tool used for cutting and shaping wood.

Sandblasting - The process of using abrasive particles to blast a surface to remove coatings, rust, or other materials.

Scratch resistance - The ability of a material to resist scratching and abrasion.

Shrinkage - The reduction in size or volume of a material during the drying or curing process.

Solvent-based - A material that contains solvents as a carrier for the active ingredients.

Stain - A substance used to color or darken wood.

Table saw - A power tool used for cutting and shaping wood.

Tensile strength - The measure of a material's resistance to breaking under tension.

Thixotropic - A material that becomes less viscous and easier to flow under stress or agitation.

Trowel - A tool used for spreading and smoothing materials like resin or concrete.

Vacuum bagging - The process of using a vacuum bag to apply pressure to a composite material to remove air bubbles and ensure a smooth surface finish.

Varnish - A transparent finish applied to wood to protect it from damage and enhance its appearance.

Warp - The distortion or bending of a material, typically caused by uneven moisture content or temperature.

Wet layup - The process of applying wet layers of composite material to a mold, typically with the use of a resin system.

Workability - The ease with which a material can be worked or shaped.

Workpiece - The piece of material being worked on or shaped, typically wood.

Yellowing - The discoloration or yellowing of a material over time, often caused by exposure to UV light.

Z-poxy - A type of two-part epoxy resin with high impact resistance and strength, commonly used for bonding and structural applications.

Adhesion - The ability of a material to stick or bond to another material.

Biocide - A substance used to kill or inhibit the growth of microorganisms.

Brushing resin - A type of resin used for coating and laminating applications, typically applied with a brush or roller.

Cellophane tape - A type of transparent tape commonly used in woodworking for masking and marking.

Chopped strand mat - A type of reinforcement material made from chopped strands of glass fibers, typically used in composite layup applications.

Epoxy coating - A type of epoxy resin used for coating surfaces to provide protection and a smooth finish.

Fracture toughness - The measure of a material's resistance to crack propagation or failure under stress.

Gelcoat - A pigmented resin used as a surface coating for composite materials to provide color and protection.

Humidity - The amount of water vapor present in the air.

Infusion - The process of using a vacuum to draw resin into a composite material to impregnate it fully.

Laminating resin - A type of resin used for laminating and bonding applications, typically with the addition of reinforcement materials.

MDF - Medium-density fiberboard, a type of engineered wood made from compressed wood fibers and resin.

Release agent - A substance used to prevent a material from sticking to a mold or surface, typically applied before the material is poured or applied.

Appreciation

Dear Reader,

Thank you for choosing **"The Ultimate Guide to Woodworking with Resin"** as your guide to exploring woodworking in combination with resin. I sincerely hope this book has provided you with valuable insights, inspiration, and practical instructions for your projects.

Please consider writing a review, if you find the information in this book helpful, scan the QR code below.

Other titles by the same author include:
- Epoxy Resin Art For Newbies
- The Comprehensive Guide to Woodworking
- How to Make Money with Woodworking
- Woodworking and Resin Art (4 Books in 1)

BOOKS BY GABRIEL ANDREWS

HOW TO MAKE
MONEY
with
WOODWORKING
Discover Hot Tips and Secrets to Selling Your Wood Crafts
GABRIEL ANDREWS

THE ULTIMATE GUIDE TO
WOODWORKING
RESIN
GABRIEL ANDREWS
EPOXY
RESIN ART
NEWBIES
WOODWORKING
AND
RESIN ART
4 BOOKS IN 1
WOODWORKING
The Beginner's Ultimate Guide to Woodworking
Gabriel Andrews
GABRIEL ANDREWS

Printed in Dunstable, United Kingdom